Awkwardness

An Essay

Awkwardness

An Essay

Adam Kotsko

BOOKS

Winchester, UK
Washington, USA

First published by O-Books, 2010
O Books is an imprint of John Hunt Publishing Ltd., The Bothy, Deershot Lodge, Park Lane, Ropley,
Hants, SO24 0BE, UK
office1@o-books.net
www.o-books.com

For distributor details and how to order please visit the 'Ordering' section on our website.

A CIP catalogue record for this book is available from the British Library.

Design: Tom Davies

Printed in the UK by CPI Antony Rowe

We operate a distinctive and ethical publishing philosophy in all
areas of its business, from its global network of authors to
production and worldwide distribution.

CONTENTS

Acknowledgments

I'd like to thank the following people for reading and commenting on my manuscript, often in multiple drafts: Ted Jennings, Natalie Scoles, Sarah Fok, Brad Johnson, Anthony Paul Smith, and Timothy Sommer. Their input was invaluable on every level, from simple factual corrections and requests for clarification all the way up to helping me to discover exactly the kind of book I was trying to write. I'd also like to thank Tariq Goddard and John Hunt of O-Books for finding a place for this strange project in the Zer0 Books series and my former roommate Michael Schaefer for subsidizing the high-end cable plan that allowed me to watch the entire series of Curb Your Enthusiasm using the "HBO On Demand" feature. Finally, I'd like to acknowledge the hospitality of Erika Bolden, who hosted a party at which I repeated my frequent claim that I was going to write a book bringing together awkwardness and Heidegger—when one of the guests jokingly responded with what was essentially an independently discovered version of one of the key points of my argument, my panic at the idea of being beaten to the punch drove me to submit a formal proposal within a matter of days.

Chapter 1

A brief introduction to the study of awkwardness

Awkwardness is everywhere, inescapable. Awkwardness dominates entertainment to such an extent that it's becoming increasingly difficult to remember laughing at anything other than cringe-inducing scenes of social discomfort. In America, apparently everyone loves seeing people cringing on *The Office*, itself based on an even more painful British original starring Ricky Gervais. Cross-cultural discomfort instigator Sacha Baron Cohen, of the TV series *Da Ali G Show* and the film *Borat*, has made yet another hidden-camera film, making straight men everywhere uncomfortable as his flamboyantly gay European character in *Brüno* ambushes them in the most unlikely places. Larry David, not content with defining 1990s irony with his classic scripts for *Seinfeld*, now inspires morbid fascination in all those who watch his social faux-pas in *Curb Your Enthusiasm*, which in its seventh season has beat out *The Sopranos* as the longest-running series on the American premium cable network HBO. More recently he has even engaged in what can only be called retro awkwardness, playing the infamous "Woody Allen character" in the film *Whatever Works*. And of course theaters are seldom without yet another movie from Judd Apatow, the champion of those who extend their awkward adolescence into their adult years and the maker of *The 40-Year-Old Virgin*, *Knocked Up*, *Superbad*, and *Pineapple Express*—or if a film by the man himself is not available, audiences can easily find one starring one of his regular ensemble of actors such as Seth Rogen or Jason Segel, or one that has no particular connection but just feels somehow Apatovian.

These are of course only a few of the most popular examples—the awkwardness trend extends much further. It embraces the free-associative and improvisational cartoons of the Adult Swim programming block on Cartoon Network, which began with the bizarre interviews between real celebrities and an apparently drug-addled cartoon character on the pseudo-talk show *Space Ghost Coast to Coast* and has continued to feature a variety of graceless fare like *Home Movies* and *Moral Orel*. It draws in more mainstream animated shows such as *The Simpsons*, *South Park*, and *Family Guy*, with their focus on the struggles of the socially inept and down-and-out. It has suffered the premature cancellation of the visionary sitcom *Arrested Development*, a show that pushes its awkwardness to the extreme of including a running gag about incest. It has seen a second show from Ricky Gervais, *Extras*, which chronicles the travails of actors hired to blend into the background and their encounters with self-absorbed stars. As the trend continues to engulf the Anglophone world, the British have, perhaps unsurprisingly, given us more awkward stars than Gervais and Baron Cohen alone, as the truly painful comedy *The Peep Show* amply illustrates. New Zealand has gotten into the act as well, as the bumbling musicians of *Flight of the Conchords* try to make their way in America. One could list many other examples: for instance, the petty schemers of *It's Always Sunny in Philadelphia* cause and experience their fair share of awkwardness, and uncomfortable scenarios abound in the UK Channel 4 sitcom *Spaced*, which follows two near-strangers posing as a couple in order to get an apartment.

Awkwardness is pervasive, and it's not limited to television or film: it stalks us everywhere. We watch awkward situations in everyday life as though we're gaping at a car accident. We are masters at diagnosing it, if not avoiding it. American adolescents, whose unevenly developing bodies give them a

2

hard-won expertise in the topic, are at the forefront here, with their simple exclamation: "Awkward!" There are self-help books for dealing with awkward co-workers, and on weekends and holidays we must deal with the awkwardness of family gatherings, where people united by blood kinship find they can't exchange even the most innocuous opinions without risking tension—and somehow the very act of withholding one's views, meant to avoid potential discomfort, itself winds up producing an awkwardness that's all too actual. Our men are awkward in seduction, always worrying that an unwelcome advance will produce impressions of awkwardness or its dread cousin creepiness, while our women never know whether making the first move will be taken as a welcome relief or an off-putting display of castrating pushiness. Our middle-class whites are absolutely hopeless when it comes to dealing with those of other cultures, wondering whether and how to note the difference, what kinds of questions to ask and not to ask—chafing at the supposed constraints of "political correctness" yet feeling very acutely the pressure to differentiate themselves from their low-class and presumably racist Caucasian confreres. And when we all come at home at night exhausted from a long day of awkwardness, what do we do but watch yet another cavalcade of awkwardness?

We live, in short, in an awkward age. We all know this on some level, all feel the awkwardness that threatens to engulf everything, all sense very acutely the terrifying possibility that civilization itself might collapse in a simultaneous worldwide cringe. We're all very concerned to develop our own strategies for avoiding or at least controlling social discomfort, and so it's perhaps understandable that so few have asked themselves what awkwardness *is*, what it means, what it's telling us about our age and about ourselves. I am among those few, drawn into the awkward project of writing a book about awkwardness after writing a joking blog post that described the phenomenon using the terminology of the German philosopher Martin Heidegger, a joke that seemed like less and less of a joke the more I thought about it.

When I decided to write a book on awkwardness, telling people about the project initially served as an all-purpose gimmick, redefining any awkward situation as "research." With one exception in this introductory chapter, however, I have chosen a method that allows me to do all my research in the comfort of my own home: watching TV shows and movies on DVD. As it turns out, I didn't even need to risk an uncomfortable encounter with a video store employee, as the Netflix DVD-rental service sends them to me by mail automatically, replacing each disc with the next entry on my queue as I ship them back using a secluded and anonymous mailbox.

My reason for choosing this arduous and lonely path is simple: we have all grown too bogged down in the *practice* of awkwardness to really focus on the *theory*. I am determined not to repeat that fatal mistake, and so my investigation in the present chapter, though beginning from the unavoidable personal experience of awkwardness, will quickly proceed to philosophical and cultural analysis. All of this will be oriented toward laying the groundwork for sharing my findings in the subsequent chapters, the research for which ultimately cost my DVD player its life—and of course it should come as no surprise that after I hooked up the DVD player my roommate had offered as a replacement, I was faced with the problem of how to deal with the pornographic movie he had left in it. Even by its very act of dying, then, my DVD player managed to bring awkwardness into my life, and it is to that faithful DVD player that I dedicate this book.

The concept of awkwardness
A pub that I frequent has a "live Irish session" on Sunday

afternoons, where instrumentalists from the music school next door play various Irish tunes. For the most part, one can proceed normally when the Irish players are in session, treating it as background music. One day, however, the instruments fell silent and a woman began singing *a capella* in a very dramatic, drawn-out, vibrato-laden style. She had had no role in the proceedings up to this point, as the music was entirely instrumental. She had apparently been just another patron sitting at the bar, and in fact she remained seated at the bar throughout the entire performance, simply turning in her seat.

The social tension that accompanied this performance was, for me at least, nearly unbearable. How, I wondered, should I handle this? Should I treat it as background music and continue my conversation accordingly? But that couldn't be right—even whispering seemed somehow rude. Should I turn toward the singer, as befitted what she is presenting as an emotion-laden and even virtuoso performance? Yet looking at her only made it worse, if such a thing was possible. And this was all complicated by the sense that even though I came to the pub knowing there would be a "live Irish session," this *a capella* segment nonetheless felt invasive and excessive, more than I or anyone else had bargained for. In fact, if anything the official endorsement of the pub made the situation more awkward—if this sudden outburst of *a capella* singing had occurred on the train, for instance, I would at least be within my rights to ask the person to stop. Here, all I could do was quietly endure.

Wherein lies the awkwardness of this situation? It's difficult to pinpoint, and our usual way of speaking about awkwardness doesn't clarify things. We might just as easily say that I feel awkward, that the singing is awkward, or that the situation as a whole is awkward. It's as though the awkwardness is continually on the move, ever present yet impossible to nail down. The etymology of the word confirms

5

this impression of movement: the *–ward* of *awkward* is the selfsame *–ward* as in *forward* or *backward*. As for the first syllable, it comes from the Middle English *awke*, which designated something turned in the wrong direction.

One might say provisionally that awkward is wrong-ward, but then what is the corresponding right-ward? If I'm described as awkward in the pub scenario, then the opposite of awkwardness would be a kind of social grace, an ability to roll with the punches when unexpected situations arise rather than being paralyzed by them. If we say that the singing is awkward, then the norm being disrupted would be the usual course of events at a pub, where background music is not suddenly replaced by a strange performance implicitly demanding the patrons' undivided attention. If the situation as a whole is what's in question, then the answer might be to keep the pub setting and the focused musical performance setting rigorously separate rather than mingling them and watching their incompatible norms collide.

These different perspectives on my situation help to get at two modes of awkwardness. First there is what I will call *everyday awkwardness*, which seems to originate with particular individuals. It combines aspects of my gracelessness and the singer's uncomfortable performance. It's difficult to deny that there are people for whom awkwardness is a kind of perverse skill, who bring it with them wherever they go. We are only able to identify someone as awkward, however, because the person does something that is inappropriate for a given context. Most often, these violations do not involve an official written law—instead, the grace that's in question is the skillful navigation of the mostly unspoken norms of a community. Severely awkward individuals are those who have particular difficulty relating to their social context, most likely due to gaps in their childhood training but in some cases also due to certain cognitive disabilities such as Asperger's Syndrome.

Even when personal deficits make certain individuals seem extremely awkward by nature, however, awkwardness remains a social phenomenon, and therefore the analysis of awkwardness should focus not on awkward individuals but on the entire social situation in which awkwardness makes itself felt.

As an initial example to support this claim, which will be central to my entire argument, consider the classical case of a joke that not only falls flat but reduces its audience to an embittered silence. Our instinct here is to put the onus on the joke-teller, who perhaps told a joke that wasn't appropriate for the setting or told it with extremely poor delivery. It should be noted, however, that the violation is two-fold insofar as the joke-teller expects at least a polite token chuckle—if the joke-teller was graceless in telling the joke in the first place, the audience is being graceless in leaving him or her out to dry. Yet wherever we choose to place the blame or whichever direction we view it from, one thing remains constant: there exists a certain norm that, though most often not explicitly stated, is regarded as both knowable and in fact known by all members of a given community. Awkwardness is then related to this stable norm as its opposite or violation.

The second mode of awkwardness that my experience with the "live Irish session" reveals is what I'll call *radical awkwardness*. In contrast to everyday awkwardness, radical awkwardness arises when there doesn't seem to be any norm governing a given situation at all. The discomfort of radical awkwardness is therefore much greater than that of everyday awkwardness, because in place of seeing one's familiar ways of navigating the world flaunted, one feels deprived of them altogether. Most often, this happens because of an encounter between two sets of norms. In my example, the encounter was the relatively innocuous one between the expectations of normal "pub" behavior and of "serious musical performance"

7

behavior, but situations of radical awkwardness involving very different cultures can often inspire reactions far more dangerous than an uncomfortable grimace, particularly when one group is significantly stronger than an other. Possibilities include forced assimilation, segregation, and expulsion, strategies that are also often at work in everyday encounters between individuals of different cultures, albeit obviously on a smaller scale. For instance, white midwestern Americans who meet someone who doesn't speak English will often attempt to make themselves understood by speaking more slowly (or worse, loudly), invoking the strategy of assimilation by assuming that *of course* the person is or should be at least attempting to learn English and simply needs a little hand-holding for now—in the process making their more enlightened peers feel awkward because of their gauche behavior.

What both everyday awkwardness and radical awkwardness share is a fundamentally *social* character. Awkwardness moves through the social network, it *spreads*. You can't observe an awkward situation without being drawn in: you are made to feel awkward as well, even if it is probably to a lesser degree than the people directly involved. In my example, the world was fortunate that the pub was a relatively enclosed area, but even then it was possible for awkwardness to spread, for instance if someone had walked in unsuspecting and been stopped cold. This property of awkwardness comes out perhaps most clearly in Ricky Gervais's original *Office*—the fact that it is so painful to watch confirmed once and for all that awkwardness can spread even by means of television. This involvement of the observer can be seen in the exclamation point of the simple adolescent proclamation "Awkward!" as well as in the interjections that almost always accompany declarations of awkwardness: "Oh God, that's awkward."

8

The participants in an awkward situation might flee the scene, but in the moment of awkwardness, they are strangely exposed, forced to share to varying degrees in the experience of awkwardness and indeed even drawing innocent bystanders into their impromptu circle. The experience of awkwardness, then, is an intrinsically social one. And this means that, paradoxically, certain violations of the norms we rely on to navigate our way through social encounters—either violating specific rules, as in everyday awkwardness, or more broadly violating our expectation that there will be rules applying to every situation, as in radical awkwardness— actually create a weird kind of social bond.

Awkwardness and philosophy

So awkwardness is not a property of a situation that could be objectively observed as though from the outside—if you are observing awkwardness *as* awkwardness, then you are drawn into the awkward situation yourself. At the same time, the spread of awkwardness makes it seem different from an emotion, which we normally think of as being located somehow inside an individual. We lack a clear word for something that is somehow between the objective and the subjective, between the status of an external situation and an emotion, a difficulty that should be unsurprising given that we're dealing with awkwardness. For the time being, we could define it as a "feeling," playing off the association with emotion and with the fact that a given situation or location can be said to have a certain "feel" to it, a certain *je ne sais quoi* in excess of the objective facts yet not easily dismissed as being all in the observer's head.

Even if I am using the word "feeling" in a non-standard way, it may nevertheless seem difficult to see how something like a feeling could be of philosophical importance. My belief that it can stems from my study of the philosophy of the

9

above-mentioned Martin Heidegger, more specifically his groundbreaking 1927 work *Being and Time*. Now Heidegger is one of the most influential philosophers of the last hundred years, and the proper interpretation of his philosophy is a matter of much dispute. In addition, he is foundational for modern European or "continental" philosophy, which has often tended to proceed by way of commentary on previous philosophers. For my purposes here, however, I believe it is possible to stick to a handful of main points that relatively few readers of Heidegger would find controversial and thereby avoid the thicket of commentary and scholarship. The opening points may seem overly abstract and irrelevant, but their significance should become clear in due course.

Heidegger's goal in *Being and Time* is to find a way to get at the question of the meaning of being. He is working in a philo-sophical tradition called phenomenology, which was founded by his teacher Edmund Husserl. In the broadest possible terms, phenomenology is concerned with getting past the preconceptions through which we approach things and letting them appear to us as they really are in themselves. An example that Heidegger uses is the progress of mathematics. It's possible to develop a lot of useful and interesting mathematics just using one's initial intuitions about what numbers are—but at a certain point, some exceptional situation will arise that causes the mathematician to stop and say, "Wait a minute, what *is* a number?" In the ancient Greek context, for example, the intuitive belief that all numbers were rational and harmo-nious was shattered by the discovery of irrational numbers like the square root of two. Similarly, one can imagine a biologist, cataloguing the forms and functions of various things that we would intuitively recognize as living beings. When a more ambiguous case such as a virus comes into view, however, it becomes necessary to ask what life really is. Heidegger believes that philosophy has historically done an adequate job of helping people to deal with those kinds of situations within particular fields. What it has not done, however, is to say, "Okay, we can clarify the nature of all these particular types of beings, but what does *being* really mean?"

In other words, philosophy has contented itself with particular beings, without grounding its efforts in a more holistic account of being in general. Now one can see that the effort to get at the meaning of being in general should probably be parallel to the attempts to clarify the meaning of particular types of beings, but the big difference between the two cases is that there doesn't seem to be a way "into" the question of being in general. In the case of particular beings like numbers, there is a more or less well-defined field within which the investigation can proceed (mathematics). Yet where can we begin when it's a matter of being in general? Heidegger's answer here is elegant: human existence. The question of what numbers are arises in mathematics, the question of what life is arises in biology, and the question of what being means arises in human existence—after all, we are the ones (apparently the only ones) who ask the question.

The place to begin, then, is an analysis of the structure of human existence. Yet this analysis cannot proceed by means of pre-given categories, such as those drawn from psychology, anthropology, or biology, which only deal with particular aspects of human existence. The categories have to be developed along the way. Heidegger begins his analysis with what he calls "ordinary everydayness," which is characterized by essentially going with the flow. I use the tools necessary for my work, I interact with others in fairly stereotyped ways, and I don't give much thought to any of it, because there's really no reason to. It's only when things start to break down that I really need to step back and reflect on what has happened. Heidegger was a very nostalgic person with a deep admiration of the supposedly "authentic" peasant lifestyle, and so he draws his examples from that milieu, in particular from the realm of the workshop. When I'm working on something in the workshop, I don't really think of a hammer, for example, as anything more than a readily available tool. It's only when it breaks that it presents itself to me as something more than just its use to me. Similarly, when I sit here typing this book in Microsoft Word, there's no need for me to ponder the logic behind the lines of code that make up the program. Only when there is an error am I prompted to try to think like the program in order to avoid the error next time.

This stance toward something that has broken down is the root of the kind of objective contemplation that philosophy and science have tended to put forward as the most authentic type of knowledge. Heidegger acknowledges that this kind of knowledge is very important and valuable, but it is already clear that it is not the only type of knowledge—there is also the kind of intuitive knowledge or "know-how" that gets us through our day-to-day life. That is to say, things present themselves differently to us depending on whether we're absorbed in some kind of task or confronted by something useless or broken. One of Heidegger's great insights is to generalize this point: human existence consists of a variety of such stances, each of which allows us to see different things. Heidegger's term for these stances has been translated as "mood," but—as when I talk about awkwardness as a "feeling"—he's not really talking about emotions in the common sense of the term. Rather, a "mood" is a certain way of standing in relationship to the world or, drawing on another translation, a way of being "attuned" to the world.

Human existence in the world is always colored by some mood or other, and there is no single overarching mood that incorporates all we can know from the other moods. Despite the lack of a "meta-mood," however, Heidegger does not believe that all moods are equally interesting or relevant for

philosophy. Some are more fundamental. The most fundamental mood he examines in the context of *Being and Time* is
anxiety, which he defines as the stance of the subject who
resolutely faces the inevitability of death. The reason anxiety
is so interesting in Heidegger's view is that it gives a special
window onto a question that he pairs with that of the meaning
of being: namely, the question of time. In ordinary everydayness, I am absorbed in a task or project that projects me
into a future in which my task will eventually be finished and
I will presumably have more tasks to carry out. In this mood,
it seems like time will go on indefinitely. Seriously facing the
inevitability of death, however, means projecting a future in
which I have no more future. When I dwell in the mood of
anxiety, time becomes more than an indifferent measurement
or an objective duration—it has an existential urgency,
because it is going to come to a definitive and irrevocable end.

Heidegger's analysis of anxiety provided a major inspi-
ration for Jean-Paul Sartre's development of existentialist
philosophy in France, and in fact one could easily get the
impression that anxiety is the *only* fundamental mood in
Heidegger's view. This is not the case, however. Although
Heidegger's later philosophy took a different direction and
left behind the more human-centered analysis of *Being and
Time*, he did produce an extended description of another
fundamental mood, namely profound boredom. (Hilariously,
the analysis of boredom, which can be found in the published
version of his seminar on *The Fundamental Concepts of
Metaphysics*, runs into the hundreds of pages.) Whereas
anxiety provides special insight into the question of time,
boredom bears specifically on the question of how humanity
is related to animal life. For Heidegger, all animals (including
humans) are drawn to certain stimuli, with more complex
animals being able to respond to a greater range of stimuli.
What makes humanity truly distinctive, however, is not that

we can handle such an amazing array of stimuli, but rather that in the mood of profound boredom we can become completely *detached* from them, completely un-energized by all the things that normally would have commanded our attention.

Up to this point, as I've said, I believe that I have limited myself to relatively non-controversial points in the interpretation of Heidegger. Now, if I am to make the case for the philosophical importance of awkwardness, I need to become more argumentative. Even here, however, I am not entering into completely uncharted territory, as I am basing my critique on the work of the contemporary French philosopher Jean-Luc Nancy. In his book *Being Singular Plural*, Nancy points out that Heidegger argues in *Being and Time* that relationship—understood in the broadest sense of our relationships to all aspects of the world, including other human beings—is fundamental to our very existence. We don't first exist and then enter into relationship, but rather are always unavoidably in relationship from the very beginning. Yet in Nancy's view and mine, Heidegger doesn't make nearly enough of this fact. Most importantly for my purposes here, although the moods that always accompany human existence are about our relationship to the world, the moods that Heidegger calls the most fundamental are about *detachment* from the world. Anxiety is about my relationship to death as my own future nothingness, and boredom is a state in which I feel strangely unenergized by my surroundings and circumstances. Ordinary everydayness, our absorption into our tasks, is about connection, but at the same time it's clear that Heidegger doesn't think that mood is worthy of much respect—one walks away from *Being and Time* thinking of everydayness as somehow inferior to the courageous stance of anxiety.

Heidegger could defend himself here by saying that his focus on the moods of anxiety and boredom follows in the general pattern of insight arising from things breaking down. Boredom is, after all, a breakdown in our normal relationship to the various stimuli we encounter in the world, and anxiety points toward the ultimate breakdown of death. For all the insight these analyses provide, however, they don't provide much of a way into the question of the meaning of *relationship*—which Heidegger himself puts forward as central to human existence. Presumably there is some mood that fits with relationship, but Nancy does not provide much help in finding it either. Though he attempts in *Being Singular Plural* to revamp Heidegger's argument in *Being and Time* by refocusing it on the question of being-with, he does not provide anything closely parallel to Heidegger's analysis of a fundamental mood.

That is the gap I propose to fill, at least partly, by putting forward awkwardness as the mood or feeling that provides the best angle on our relationships with other people, or the intrinsically social nature of humanity. Awkwardness clearly fits with the general pattern of insight through breakdown, but unlike anxiety or boredom, it doesn't isolate the person who feels awkward—as I have already discussed, it does just the opposite: it spreads. In this regard, it follows the pattern set by Heidegger's other fundamental moods. Just as anxiety is a breakdown in our normal experience of time yet still involves time and boredom is a breakdown in our normal relationship to stimuli yet is still defined by stimuli (in their very absence), so also awkwardness is a breakdown in our normal experience of social interaction while itself remaining irreducibly social.

Taking it a step further, in Heidegger's examples, the breakdown of the norm gives us access to a more fundamental level that helps to explain our everyday experience. In the case of anxiety, the reality of death is what drives us to take on projects. If time really did just continue indefinitely, there would be no hurry to do anything at any particular time because we could just do it later. It doesn't require a major stretch of the imagination to see that a race of immortal humans would therefore do nothing at all. The fact that time will end for me is what makes time meaningful. In the case of boredom, the fact that we are able to detach from all stimuli means that we are not irrevocably bound to any particular stimulus, and therefore that our ability to block out all stimuli is paradoxically what grounds our ability to pay attention to essentially anything we come across—from food and sexual partners to black holes and microbes.

Following the pattern, one could say that the tension of awkwardness indicates that no social order is self-evident and no social order accounts for every possibility. Awkwardness shows us that humans are fundamentally social, but that they have no built-in norms: the norms that we develop help us to "get by," with some proving more helpful than others. We might say, then, that awkwardness is what prompts us to set up social norms in the first place—and what prompts us to transform them.

The idea that social orders are always provisional and incomplete was already implicit in my discussion of everyday awkwardness—after all, if the social order really did have a regulation prepared for every encounter, awkwardness would never occur in the first place. Everyday awkwardness happens in a context where the social order seems more or less adequate and comfortable, but the provisional nature of every social order indicates that it's not an all-or-nothing question of either having a social order or none, as in the opposition between everyday and radical awkwardness, between awkwardness in violation of a social norm and awkwardness in the absence of a social norm. I propose that there is a particularly awkward kind of awkwardness in between the two, which I will call *cultural awkwardness*. It arises when there seems to be a set of norms in force, but it feels somehow impossible to follow them or even fully know them. Just as it is easier to criticize than to create something, a social order in decline maintains its ability to tell you what you're doing wrong even as it is losing its ability to provide a convincing account of what it would look like to do things right. Gene Hackman's character in *The Royal Tenenbaums* captures this Kafkaesque dynamic well when he says, "It's certainly frowned upon, but then, what isn't these days?"

Putting the three on a continuum, one could say that *everyday awkwardness* names the violation of a relatively strong norm, *cultural awkwardness* the general malaise that accompanies a relatively weak norm, and *radical awkwardness* the panic brought on by the lack of any norm at all.

The origins of an awkward age

It should be clear by this point that I believe that we are currently in a state of cultural awkwardness. Contemporary mainstream middle-class social norms are not remotely up to the task of minimizing awkwardness, but at the same time, there seems to be no real possibility of developing a convincing positive alternative. There are many possible reasons that such a condition could have arisen in the first decade of the 21st century—the apparently ontological awkwardness of George W. Bush comes to mind—but to trace the origins of our current uncomfortable state, I believe we must look to the social upheavals of the 1960s. My account here is going to be focused primarily on American culture in the postwar era, a move that I hope is at least somewhat justified in view of the leading role America has increasingly taken in global popular culture. Tracing shifts in expectations about family life, cross-cultural relations, and work, I will argue that the failure to develop a stable vision to replace the so-called "traditional values" that the 1960s era rightly called into radical question has meant that the festering wound of cultural awkwardness has never healed, with the decades that followed offering makeshift solutions at best.

The social upheaval of the 1960s must be understood in terms of the era that preceded it. The political and economic system that emerged in the United States and other Western nations in the aftermath of World War II has been called Fordism. Broadly speaking, it relied on cooperation among business, labor, and government actors, emphasized stability over rapid growth, and led to a steady and broadly-shared increase in standards of living. As indicated by the era's name, the automobile was a huge factor, as the auto industry provided economic leadership and car-based suburbs reshaped the nation's landscape.

A big part of what made this system possible was the perceived need to combat the Soviet Union by showing that a capitalist economy could produce a just prosperity, a propaganda effort that went hand-in-hand with the endorsement of "traditional Christian values"—most notably the patriarchal family and the ideal of a submissive and attentive stay-at-home mother—over against communist atheism. Not everything was in line with the propaganda effort, however. Most importantly, there was the oppression of blacks that flatly contradicted the ideal of freedom and equality, legally enforced in the south but still strong in other parts of the country—the most significant cross-cultural relationship in American history, that between blacks and whites, had for the time being settled into a firm hierarchy.

Fordism was, in sum, a seemingly very stable system based on a growing (white) middle class, centered on a nuclear family headquartered in a suburban home. By the mid-1960s, however, it became clear that there were significant problems that the system was essentially ignoring. The oppression of African-Americans and the dissatisfaction of educated women forced into homemaker roles were among the most serious, while the rolling catastrophe of the Vietnam War inspired a more generalized rebellion. The "sexual revolution" emerged along with an experimental drug culture, and acts of revolt worldwide convinced many that a wholesale restructuring of society was only a matter of time.

The results, as everyone now knows, were mixed at best. The African-American civil rights movement and feminist movement both achieved considerable gains, but more radical changes proved elusive as the forces of cultural conservatism turned out to retain considerable power. It is here, I claim, that we find the ultimate origin of contemporary awkwardness: the events of the 1960s threw the normative social model significantly off-kilter, making it impossible to embrace that model wholeheartedly—and yet they did not produce any viable positive alternative. The idea that a woman's place was in the home and that African-Americans occupied a lower rung on the social hierarchy was no longer self-evident, yet it was—and even today remains—unclear what concrete steps one should take to fully acknowledge and actualize their equality. It is from this tension that there emerged the experimentation but also the paranoia and occasional nihilism of 1970s culture, and it is no accident, I believe, that Woody Allen, truly one of the pioneers of awkwardness, emerged as a serious filmmaker in the 1970s.

By the 1970s, awkwardness, not the stability of Fordism, had become the new "default setting" of American culture. The basic economic system of Fordism remained largely in place, albeit with a tenuous hold, but the civil rights movement had upset the always unstable relationship between blacks and whites and emboldened other minority groups as well, while feminism seriously disrupted expectations about marriage, family life, and the coming of age they represented. It was perhaps this awkwardness, and even more the lack of energy for a creative effort to develop new norms to overcome it, that Jimmy Carter was getting at when he pointed out what everyone knew and no one wanted to admit: America was in a malaise. The conservative movement that hit its stride with the election of Ronald Reagan in 1980s represents, among other things, an attempt to overcome this awkwardness with the assertion of unfettered capitalism as a positive ethos, legitimated by an appeal to the specter of "traditional American values" and a belligerent anti-communism. The middle class white Americans who formed a part of Nixon's "silent majority" were, in theory at least, no longer confused about the direction they were heading: they were fighting the Evil Empire by adhering to the deep moral insight that "greed is good."

In a bait-and-switch that would become standard operating procedure for the American right, the very people who mobilized resentment against the loss of the traditional values associated with Fordism were undercutting the economic base that made those aspirations possible. Financial deregulation combined with deindustrialization became the norm, undermining the power of labor unions and producing increasing economic inequality — patterns that would persist for the next 30 years. As one who grew up around the environs of Flint, Michigan, formerly the home of General Motors and now most famous for the rapid decline captured in Michael Moore's documentary *Roger & Me*, I can testify that the consequences of this shift were devastating. Maintaining the American dream of a secure family home in the suburbs, even leaving aside the ideal of maintaining a submissive stay-at-home wife, is simply impossible in the face of such economic ruin. Meanwhile, the feminist goal of fully incorporating women into public life and therefore the workplace found its perverse realization in the increasing necessity for both partners to work regardless of their opinion of the traditional family structure. At the same

20

time, aspirations toward black self-determination had found their own perverse answer in the form of "white flight" to suburban areas, abandoning blacks to cities that now had no tax base and were therefore in apparently terminal decline.

Despite these huge challenges, there were noteworthy victories for civil rights during this period. Yet arguably the only concrete progress toward a holistic positive social vision came in the attempt to develop respectful ways of talking across various cultural lines, a trend mercilessly pilloried by the right as "political correctness." These well-intentioned guidelines had a major disadvantage from my standpoint: given that they were such recent creations, they couldn't help but feel unnatural and therefore awkward, even to those who sympathized with their goals. This problem was exacerbated by the tendency for the newly-coined terms to become vehicles for the same derision attached to the terms they replaced, leading to a seemingly endless procession of new acceptable terms and a state of constant confusion as to the proper term to use at any given time. The decline of the old racial hierarchy had led to a new uncertainty as to how to interact across the cultural line separating whites from others, and now the proposed solution only seemed to make the problem worse.

Based on the narrative thus far, one would expect that with the end of the "evil empire," American culture, deprived of its transcendent mission, would collapse back into awkwardness. After all, capitalism, founded as it is in greed, is difficult to take seriously as a positive moral ethos in the absence of a "more evil" opponent. What happened instead, however, was a movement toward what is known as "irony." Taking the linguistic meaning of "irony" as saying what one doesn't really mean, exponents of 90s-style irony created a more general stance of detachment from life in general—a stance of somehow not "meaning" whatever it is that they were doing.

An example of this kind of irony that persists even today is the tendency for young people to "ironically" wear clothes that are widely acknowledged as tacky, out of the belief that doing so is somehow witty.

I would propose that the turn toward irony, which amounts ultimately to an escapism, has economic roots. The baseline understanding of family life and race relations had been shattered long ago, but it was only in the 1980s that the same kind of awkwardness took a leading role in the workplace as well. The idea that a blue-collar worker could enjoy a comfortable middle-class existence — the core promise of Fordism — seemed increasingly to be a fantasy, and the new mainstream middle-class jobs were of a vaguely "white collar" kind, not quite professional (though demanding "profession-alism") and certainly not as secure as the traditional unionized factory jobs. The 1990s "tech boom," with its creed that the economy could become increasingly virtual, was of a piece with this increasingly disembodied work. Most office workers from that time forward could probably relate to the sputtering and defensive non-answer to the consultant's pointed question in the late-90s classic *Office Space*: "What is it that you'd say *you do here?*"

In this context, we can see why the cultural emblem of the 1990s is *Seinfeld*. Co-created by Larry David and Jerry Seinfeld, this "show about nothing" is based in Seinfeld's so-called "observational humor," which basically consists of encouraging the audience to assume a detached and bemused stance toward even the most obvious everyday realities — to make up an example: "What's the deal with socks? I mean, come on!" It follows the misadventures of Jerry Seinfeld, his best friend George Costanza, his ex-girlfriend Elaine Benes, and his oddball neighbor Kramer as they deal with everyday irritations in New York City.

To the question of what it is the characters do, the answer is for the most part "nothing." George, for example, is for most of the series an unemployed loser living with his parents, while Kramer has no apparent means of support at all. Jerry makes his living as a comedian and Elaine works in publishing, but these jobs are no obstacle to spending hours a day in a coffee shop or lounging about in Jerry's apartment. Their selfishness does lead them to undertake petty schemes that wind up alienating virtually everyone they come in contact with, yet theirs is a very strange kind of selfishness in that it's not grounded in any apparent goal or quest for advantage—they are detached from the consequences of their actions just as they are detached from everything. An elaborate plot can be dropped at a moment's notice (including at one point a plan for Jerry and Elaine to marry), revealing that their activities are all little more than defenses against boredom. From this perspective, the oft-derided series finale is actually a work of genius, providing the only possible conclusion: as punishment for their selfish and destructive deeds, the gang is condemned essentially to continue as normal, with the slight change of being in prison.

At this point, a reader might object that *Seinfeld* is in fact awkward. I will concede that there are frequent awkward moments, but I don't think that awkwardness is anything like the guiding principle of the show. Socially uncomfortable moments are not dwelt upon, but become material for either detached bemusement or petty scheming, as does essentially everything in the *Seinfeld* cast's lives. None of the main characters actually sit and stew in their awkwardness, and I'd propose that that's because they are all essentially sociopaths. They cause awkwardness in others but don't truly feel it themselves, because they lack any real investment in the social order—instead, they merely attempt to manipulate it. The one possible exception here is George, a character who was based on Larry David. His sheer patheticness and vulnerability, his lack of the steady income and social status of Jerry or Elaine or the strange self-assurance of Kramer, keep him from being completely detached. More broadly, though, I'd propose that it's possible that *Seinfeld*'s ironic detachment provided a kind of necessary cushion to prepare us for our later cultural embrace of awkward humor. Viewed from this perspective, the show gives us a safe distance from which to get used to awkwardness. In addition, it gradually weans us off our desire to see awkward situations resolved, due to its characteristic gesture of ending an episode in mid-catastrophe. The seeds of the awkwardness trend are thus planted here, but they won't fully bloom until Larry David's own show *Curb Your Enthusiasm*.

Though it was for a time quite fashionable to claim that the terrorist attacks of September 11, 2001, marked "the end of irony," I would propose a more straightforward explanation: the irony trend simply exhausted itself. The exhaustion hypothesis has the advantage of actually explaining what followed the "end of irony": not, as the 9/11 fetishists would have it, a culture-wide turn toward earnestness and patriotism, but rather a reemergence of the awkwardness that I have claimed as the "default setting" of American culture since the 1970s. As we will see, 90s-style irony even today remains an important part of many people's defense against awkwardness, but it is now mainly a temporary expedient rather than an all-encompassing lifestyle choice. In the cases where something like irony has played a dominant role, it has tended to shade into a more obvious sociopathy, as in *It's Always Sunny in Philadelphia*, which can be understood as a radical reworking of *Seinfeld* for a post-irony era.

To summarize, then: awkwardness arose in the aftermath of the social upheaval of the 1960s, becoming firmly established in the 1970s. The attempt in the 1980s to put forward unfettered capitalism as an inherent good fell apart once the fall of communism deprived capitalism of its moral gravitas, resulting in the turn toward a pure escapism based in so-called "irony" in the 1990s. By the turn of the millennium, irony—which didn't even attempt to produce any kind of positive ethos—had completely run out of steam and American culture found itself back in the throes of a thorough-going awkwardness. And in a promising move, the awkwardly nameless first decade of the new millennium witnessed the emergence of a sitcom known as *That 70s Show* as a major hit, while the attempted sequel *That 80s Show* fell completely flat—an early sign that we were perhaps finally ready to deal with our collective awkwardness head-on, without recourse to the failed solutions of the 1980s.

Awkward, but in a good way

My goal in this book is not to put forward the holistic social vision that would provide us with the relatively strong set of norms necessary to minimize awkwardness. The cultural awkwardness that afflicts us may well have pushed us past the point of no return, the point at which other societies throughout history have become strongly tempted by the fascist promise of a clear set of values and expectations and have found themselves willing to live with the inevitably tragic means used to establish those norms. Partly in light of that danger, my goal is to make a case in favor of awkwardness, arguing that it holds a certain promise and that in some cases radical awkwardness can be a good thing, not only something we can tolerate but something we can embrace.

In order to get to this counterintuitive conclusion, I will be employing the dialectical form of argument, most commonly associated with the name of another German philosopher, G. W. F. Hegel. At its root the dialectical method proceeds by starting with a seemingly obvious position, then searching for its inherent flaws, which give rise to another possible answer.

I will be tracing my way through the three cultural settings I identified as being most shaken up in the wake of the 1960s—work, family structures (and coming of age), and cross-cultural relations—in parallel with my three types of awkwardness—everyday, cultural, and radical—showing in each case how an exemplary television show or group of films illustrates the self-undermining stances toward awkwardness that I will be outlining in short order. My investigation of everyday awkwardness in the context of work will focus on *The Office*, in both its original and US versions. For the cultural awkwardness associated with the problem of family life and coming of age, I will look at the films of Judd Apatow, centered as they are on the travails of "overgrown adolescents." Finally, for the radical awkwardness represented first of all by cross-cultural tensions, I will look at Larry David's *Curb Your Enthusiasm*. Naturally there are many other options that I could have chosen, but I believe that these examples are particularly helpful ways into the argument I want to make—and they also happen to be cultural products I really enjoy.

My argument starts from a very commonly-held position people take in explaining everyday awkwardness, namely that awkwardness is caused by particularly awkward individuals—get rid of them and the awkwardness would disappear with them. This is the position, I believe, that is represented by the US version of *The Office*. This explanation of awkwardness can't be right, however, because awkwardness is intrinsically social and therefore can't be limited to particular individuals. Awkward people are always awkward in relationship to a particular context, and this brings us to the seed of doubt detectable in the original UK *Office*: what if some social orders, such as the modern workplace, actually *produce* certain forms of awkward behavior? This suspicion marks the transition from everyday to cultural awkwardness.

The second position describes a common way of dealing

with cultural awkwardness. Namely, if the social order itself somehow seems to be producing awkwardness, let people indulge in awkwardness on purpose as a way of letting off steam. This strategy is on full display in several Judd Apatow films: if men are afraid to leave behind the awkward state of overgrown adolescence and get married, then build in a space for them to indulge in their awkwardly adolescent pleasures. Here again there arises a seed of doubt: the social order is supposed to protect us against awkwardness. How, then, can things get turned upside down, such that we are promised our allowance of awkwardness if we mostly go with the flow of society? In other words: if what we really want is awkwardness, why have a social order at all?

The answer given is that the radical awkwardness produced by the total lack of a governing social norm is simply too much for anyone to endure. Many of the scenarios of cross-cultural awkwardness in *Curb Your Enthusiasm* certainly seem to bear out this claim. Yet at least a few of them contain a final seed of doubt, pointing toward the possibility that there is a good kind of awkwardness that is not defined, either positively or negatively, by the social order. If there is, then the overgrown adolescents have a point—there is something good, something promising, about awkwardness—but don't go far enough. When we resist awkwardness, the social order looks good. When we resist the social order, awkwardness looks good. But on those rare occasions when we figure out a way to stop resisting the social order and yet also stop resisting awkwardness and just *go with it*, something genuinely new and unexpected might happen: we might be able to simply enjoy one another without the mediation of any expectations or demands.

That, I believe, is the promise of awkwardness. For all its admitted perils and difficulties, awkwardness does contain a seed of hope. We testify to that hope, albeit mostly unconsciously, every time we laugh at awkwardness, and we show that we long for the fulfillment of that hope every time we take the bizarre step of voluntarily subjecting ourselves to it. More than describing a cultural trend, then, my goal here is ultimately to point toward what we're all already hoping for.

Chapter 2

Everyday awkwardness—*The Office*

Work seems like an especially promising place to investigate everyday awkwardness. On the one hand, there is, at least in theory, an unusually clear set of expectations in most workplaces: tasks to be carried out, employee handbooks to adhere to, and a full-time referee (the manager) to make sure that everyone is interpreting the directives in the same way. On the other hand, there is widespread agreement that awkward coworkers are a common problem, inspiring both a considerable self-help literature and, more importantly for my purposes, driving the success of Ricky Gervais and Stephen Merchant's BBC "mockumentary" *The Office* and its many foreign adaptations, the American version of which had begun its sixth season at the time of this writing. On the surface, *The Office* appears to take my opening position of blaming workplace awkwardness on intrinsically awkward individuals, or on situations that seem extrinsic to the office environment as such, most notably romantic tension. This is the aspect of the show that the American version most picks up on, and I will focus bringing out the internal contradictions that point toward the possibility that the contemporary white-collar workplace is inherently awkwardness-inducing. This latter position is brought out most clearly in the original series, above all—and apparently paradoxically—in the character of David Brent, the manager who at first glance seems to personify the intrinsically awkward individual most often blamed for workplace awkwardness. In the end, I will argue, *The Office* portrays the modern workplace as bogged down in a condition of cultural awkwardness.

Dealing with awkward co-workers

"You're not that awful boss, are you?" So ends yet another chapter in David Brent's dispiriting attempts to find a date for the Christmas party of the company from which he's been fired. The lead character in the original British version of the *Office*, played by Ricky Gervais, certainly is an "awful boss." The manager of the Slough office of the fictional Wernham Hogg paper company, he's bad at his job in the most direct sense, displaying such a complete lack of management skill that the audience begins to wonder how he ever got promoted in the first place, or indeed why his office was chosen for the "documentary" that provides the frame for the show.

More importantly, however, David is "awful" on a personal level, continually abusing his position. It's not really corruption that's at issue here. His greatest sin in that regard is hiring a personal secretary when the company is laying off workers, choosing among the candidates based solely on attractiveness. Rather, he abuses his position in a more innocuous and pathetic way, using it as a vehicle for his massive ego. Convinced that he is a veritable polymathic genius, David believes that his subordinates view him as a kind of mentor or even father figure and that his endless barrage of lame jokes works as a morale-booster. His attempts at humor do sometimes take a cruel turn. Perhaps the most notable example is the final scene of the pilot episode, when he calls in the receptionist, Dawn, to tell her that she's fired—only once she has started sobbing does he tell her he's joking, apparently expecting her to crack up. Even this example, however, is basically a product of a lack of self-awareness so radical that it comes to seem a willful self-delusion. That self-delusion reaches its fever point in the final installment of the series, from which my opening example is drawn. Set after the documentary that the first two seasons supposedly represented has aired, the finale finds David fired from Wernham

Hogg and trying to capitalize on the notoriety the series has gained him, even though he admits that he comes off as a complete ass (in his mind, due to malicious editing).

In short, David Brent is what one might call a uniquely awkward person, the kind of guy whose very presence is wince-inducing and whose every utterance is painful. Yet though David is the center of *The Office*'s awkward comedy, it would be a mistake to view him as the cause of all of his workplace's awkwardness. There are certainly other characters who appear to be more or less intrinsically awkward, such as David's assistant and lackey Gareth, an over-serious and ghoulish-looking man who derives endless pride from his service in the Territorial Army (the UK equivalent of the US National Guard). But arguably the greatest source of awkwardness aside from David is the romantic tension between two people who seem perfectly normal: Dawn, the aforementioned receptionist, and Tim, a good-natured salesman who is also Gareth's desk mate. The two bond through playing childish pranks on Gareth, both physical pranks like cooking his stapler in a Jell-O mold and verbal pranks that mainly center on asking leading questions whose answers make Gareth sound gay.

Despite this childishness, their relationship is obviously very meaningful to both Dawn and Tim, serving as a respite from their disappointing lives. Tim still lives with his parents at age thirty, always intending to go back to school but afraid to let go of a job he considers pointless. Dawn has also exchanged her dreams for safety, giving up on her ambition to be an illustrator for children's books and stoically enduring her unfulfilling relationship with her fiancé Lee, an insensitive man who works in the Wernham Hogg warehouse adjoining the office. Their romance produces many uncomfortable moments, but arguably the most cringe-worthy comes after Dawn confides in Tim about some problems she's been having with Lee and he mistakenly believes that the two have split up—he accordingly asks her out on a date in full view of the office, only to be turned down. Another moment that is perhaps more properly tense than awkward comes when Lee catches Tim flirting with Dawn and pushes him against the wall.

In both of these examples, it seems clear that in contrast to David Brent's apparent ontological awkwardness, the source of the awkwardness is the intrusion of something inappropriate or foreign into the workplace: romance and violence, respectively. In all these cases, then, one is tempted to claim that if you removed the intrusion—if David were fired, for example, or Tim and Dawn saved it for after work—then the office would experience a smooth, non-awkward functioning. This very same presupposition seems to be at work in the extant self-help literature about dealing with awkward co-workers: the problem is particular strange individuals, without whom things would proceed quite comfortably. One could even argue that the very frame of the show as a "mockumentary" biases the presentation toward awkwardness, as the cameras and we the viewers are implicitly intruding on and therefore somehow disturbing even the most innocuous scene.

What makes the original *Office* so interesting to me, however, is the way that it challenges this common-sense notion and lays bear the uncomfortable truth that the modern white-collar workplace is inherently and irreducibly awkward. It is unsurprising that a British show should serve as the messenger here. Though my analysis in the previous chapter was US-centric, the same forces of neoliberalism that transformed the American Fordist workplace into the vague and uncertain environment we now know have also hit the UK, indeed even earlier and to an even greater degree. That underlying economic reality may well account partly for the much greater harshness of the original UK *Office* when compared to the later US version—yet the gap in quality is much greater than the gap between the experience of workers in the US and UK, indicating that cultural factors are at work as well. The mainstream of American comedy has nearly always been "comedy" in the strict classical sense of requiring a happy ending and has too seldom given a place to the deep hopelessness that leavens so much of the best English comedy. The result in the present case is that while the US *Office* works fairly well as entertainment, it fails to get at the more profound experience of awkwardness that one finds in the original. For that reason, it seems best to examine the US version first, the better to set in relief the achievements of the original British version.

Awkwardness and irony in the workplace

The US version of *The Office*, developed by Greg Daniels, was initially based around the same core of four characters as in Gervais and Merchant's original, altered to varying degrees for an American audience. The most similar to their UK counterparts are the star-crossed lovers Pam and Jim, who start off in essentially the same place as Dawn and Tim in the original—bonding through pranks played on the Gareth-equivalent, their relationship stymied by Pam's long engagement to a warehouse worker. Gareth is replaced by Dwight, a hyper-motivated and power-hungry salesman. Drawing on Gareth's fascination with the military, the writers make Dwight into a kind of survivalist and aspiring "MacGyver" character who uses his position as safety monitor to force his co-workers into increasingly contrived drills. The element of skill and effectiveness is the main change from Gareth to Dwight: not only is Dwight the leading salesman in the office while Gareth appears to do nothing whatsoever, but the audience suspects (or at least I suspect) that, in contrast to Gareth's clearly empty talk, Dwight actually does possess the strange survivalist-type skills he frequently claims.

This change also produces a change in Dwight's relationship to his boss. He is still a lackey, in this case because of a deep-seated love of the Dunder-Mifflin paper company that results in an exaggerated belief in its hierarchy, but he often appears to be cultivating a favored son status in order to gain authority for himself. This desire for power, which leads him to flaunt his made-up title of "assistant regional manager" (or "assistant *to* the regional manager," as his boss insists on calling him in what is arguably the least funny running gag in the history of television), also makes him seem much more deserving of lampooning than his British equivalent Gareth, who is basically weird but harmless. Here already, there is a bias toward the supposed intrinsic awkwardness of individuals, to the detriment of the awkwardness of the workplace environment as such.

The biggest change is in the central character, manager Michael Scott. The first season begins with what seems like an attempt at a very close parallel with David Brent, but Michael quickly becomes more of a loveable buffoon. Many have claimed that this is a concession to the American audience, but David Brent also became more sympathetic over time. What's more, the huge success enjoyed by *House M.D.* leads me to believe that Americans can actually handle a series with an unsympathetic lead character. A more likely explanation, it seems to me, is that the choice of Steve Carell to play Michael influenced the character. Carell is a veteran of awkward humor, co-writing and starring in Judd Apatow's film *The 40-Year Old Virgin* in the same year that his *Office* character debuted (2005), after several years as a bumbling correspondent on the fake news program *The Daily Show*. All this experience must have made him seem a natural choice to star in an adaption of one of the most awkward shows of all time — yet his particular brand of awkwardness is very different from that of the David Brent character. In place of self-delusion and over-confidence, Carell cultivates an exaggerated reserve and a cluelessness that produces frequent non-sequiturs. Here one thinks of his role in the 2004 Will Ferrell vehicle *Anchorman*, where Carell plays a weatherman with an IQ of 48 who is, appropriately enough, named Brick.

Due to Carell's influence, Michael Scott becomes increasingly unbelievable on every level. Whereas one could picture a confident go-getter like David Brent somehow falling into a management position and then abusing it, Michael Scott, despite a few flashes of brilliance in the early seasons, most often seems to have an actual mental disability that is immediately evident to everyone he comes in contact with. David should obviously not be put in a position of power over other people, but Michael should not be allowed to operate an oven. Nevertheless, Michael continually succeeds where David fails, above all in romantic pursuits. David continually clashes with his female superior, who is outraged by his unprofessional behavior; Michael has a long affair with his. David's ham-fisted attempts at flirting with new female employees get him nowhere; Michael strikes up an instant romance with the first suitable candidate who sparks his interest (Holly, played by *The Wire*'s Amy Ryan). On the job front, David ends up fired after two short seasons, whereas Michael has managed to hold down his job through five much longer seasons—in fact, after he quits in the fifth season due to feeling underappreciated (!) and starts his own paper company to compete with Dunder-Mifflin, he eventually winds up being bought out and rehired to his former position.

Perhaps this inexplicable charm is meant to give credence to the claim that he was a great salesman before being inappropriately promoted to manager. Yet for me it helps to get at the major flaw in the US series: the pervasive sense that the primary cause of awkwardness in the workplace is the presence of intrinsically awkward individuals like Michael or Dwight or any of the other supporting characters that the US show's more expansive format has allowed it to introduce and explore.

The romance between Pam and Jim provides another angle on this problem. Where the original *Office* made Dawn and Tim's declaration of love a triumphant conclusion, the US version's longer run has faced it with the choice of either continuing the tension forever or consummating the relationship in the middle of the series. The latter choice is always risky, as there are very few examples of a sitcom based on sexual tension resolving that tension without ruining everything. That is the path the US *Office* took with Pam and Jim, however, and I think the writers have done reasonably well under the circumstances, perhaps because the wider range of developed characters allows them to introduce other budding office romances to fill the gap. What interests me in this relationship, however, is not how well it deals with one of the major formal problems of the sitcom genre, but the way in which it portrays awkwardness as a fixable problem. This is especially true in the case of Jim, who is generally presented as a baseline cool (non-awkward) person made awkward by his unrequited love for Pam. Once that tension is resolved, he moves fluently through the workplace, toying with his oddball co-workers from a detached distance.

Now Tim and Jim are both intended to be sympathetic "everyman" characters and therefore to serve as a point of identification for the audience that their respective bosses cannot supply. Yet the later detachment of Jim makes him a stand-in for the audience in a weirdly recursive way by turning him into a kind of internal spectator. His interactions with other co-workers, especially Dwight, often cause awkwardness, but he does it intentionally for his own enjoyment, just as the audience members intentionally subject themselves to awkwardness due to its humor value. Though his relationship with Pam ties him to the office on a personal level, the relationship's consummation makes him a kind of insider-outsider with regard to its awkwardness, which he only experienced by means of his unrequited love. Further dispelling the awkwardness, the writers mostly leave aside the rather obvious option of making the office relationship awkward in itself—the other characters don't seem to care one way or another, and Pam and Jim are so comfortable with the idea of their relationship playing out in the workplace that they are positively eager to fulfill the requirement of reporting their involvement to the human resources department.

On a common-sense level, Jim's escape from awkwardness makes sense: the source of tension is removed, and his strange office environment can then become a kind of "new normal." What's more, it seems to cut against my claim that the modern white collar workplace is somehow inherently awkward. I contend, however, that Jim hasn't escaped awkwardness at all. Instead, he has done nothing more than return to 90's-style irony. In contrast to the *Seinfeld* cast's sociopathic detachment from all aspects of life, Jim's irony is limited to the workplace—he is a devoted and even sentimental boyfriend (and later husband). Yet his strategy is every bit as unstable as it proved to be in the 90's, as the writers show in a very satisfying plot arc surrounding the introduction of a new character: Vice President for Regional Sales Charles Minor (Idris Elba, who also played Stringer Bell in *The Wire*).

A no-nonsense businessman, Charles has no patience for Jim's pranks and quickly comes to the conclusion that Jim is an idiot. In one of the most awkward scenes in the US series, Jim wears a tuxedo to work, knowing that his debonair appearance will cause Michael to take his ideas more seriously than Dwight's, thereby fulfilling his constant goal of making Dwight frustrated. When Charles walks into a meeting among the three and asks why Jim is wearing a tuxedo, however, the normally cool and composed Jim is reduced to mumbling excuses that Charles clearly finds ridiculous. Jim later tries to gain favor with Charles by feigning a shared interest in soccer, but that attempt backfires when Charles challenges him to a game—not only does Jim prove to be an incompetent soccer player, but he also causes the injury of another co-worker when he frantically ducks out of the ball's path. Suddenly the detached manipulator can do nothing right.

Eventually Charles lightens up, but the fact that a single change in his environment reduced Jim to full-fledged awkwardness shows how fragile the solution of irony is—and in an example of the pre-90's, dictionary-definition type of irony, it is Jim's very solution to the problem of awkwardness that produces the awkward tension with Charles. Even more importantly, it opens up the possibility that the workplace is an inherently awkward environment, because Jim wouldn't need a strategy for avoiding awkwardness in the first place if he really had solved the problem by finally getting together with Pam.

For me, this plot arc represents the best of the American *Office*, a moment when the show seems to transcend its limitations and deal with awkwardness in a rigorous way. Yet even in this case, it returns to familiar paths. It would have been sufficient for Charles's stay at the office to come to an end and things to return to normal for Jim, but the writers take it a step further with a volleyball match at the company picnic where Charles is revealed to be an over-competitive bully. While the earlier soccer match had hinted in this direction, for the most part it had seemed that Charles was the very pinnacle of a cool and non-awkward person, the kind of person who "just does his job"—but it turns out that he was an inherently awkward person all along and perhaps even felt somehow threatened by Jim. The problem was Charles personally, then, not the disruption his arrival produced and certainly not the inherent awkwardness of the manager-employee relationship: in true American style, it's the individual and not the system that's to blame.

What do I hate when I hate my job?

Asking the original *Office* to speak to systemic problems may seem like a stretch, since its story is so much about individuals: the fall of David Brent, the romance between Tim and Dawn. Yet the inherent problems of white collar work are always lurking in the background. It's not simply the continual problem of job insecurity, which hangs over the first season in particular—with everyone using that wonderfully euphemistic British term "redundancies," which gives one the impression that through some clerical error an excessive number of workers happen to have been hired and management is simply correcting the problem. In this connection, we could say that the American equivalent "layoffs" points to a difference in national character, implying that one is temporarily released into a kind of reserve workforce and may hope to be called back up again.

Naturally, neither nation's management class is particularly inclined to use the straightforward term "firings." The obscurantist management-speak, however, may be getting at something despite itself: there does seem to be something different about losing one of these vague white collar office jobs as opposed to a classical Fordist job or a true professional career. Tim's attitude is exemplary here. Always convinced that he's going to go back to school, he goes so far as to refuse a promotion because it would make things seem too permanent. The worker comes to view the company in the same instrumental way the company views him or her, as opposed to the presumed lifetime relationship—and therefore identity—that Fordism or the professions offered. They are all simply biding their time until their real dream becomes feasible. The pattern is very familiar, and it is not limited to any particular era: for instance, the protagonist of Thomas Hardy's *Jude the Obscure*, published in 1895, is a stonemason who's "really" an aspiring academic.

What is unique about the present era's vaguely white collar office work, however, is that it is almost impossible to imagine anyone fully identifying with it. And the reason is that there is ultimately nothing to identify *with*. No one has the answer to the *Office Space* consultant's insistent question: "What is it that you'd say *you do here*?" This is especially the case with the setting for the *Office*, namely, the sales office for a paper company. What they're selling is blank, at best providing the opportunity for someone else to do something at a later time — just as the workers themselves are biding their time until they can really do something. People do work, of course. They talk on the phone, make copies, and make appointments, yet the whole thing seems like an act. We never see the actual sales taking place, so everything appears to be the proverbial attempt to "look busy."

It's this sense of going through the motions rather than truly identifying with and relying on a set of stable norms that makes the workplace a setting of cultural awkwardness rather than simple everyday awkwardness. Here the romance plotline provides a nice counterpoint: during a period when Tim feels particularly burned by his failed attempts to win Dawn's heart, he becomes extraordinarily hardworking and businesslike in what seems like an attempt to punish her by depriving her of her fun office friend. It's a special case of a more general act.

Losing this type of job is obviously a very serious matter in economic terms, but there is always a twinge of relief — the type of relief that comes with being caught in an elaborate scam and no longer having to keep up appearances. Media reports about the collapse of Bernie Madoff's massive pyramid scheme in late 2008 imparted an air of mystery to his motives for voluntarily confessing, but surely everyone who has wiled away hours on the internet at work, while keeping Microsoft Excel running in the background and quickly switching to it when someone walked by, can relate to what he must have been feeling. The Fordist worker may have rhetorically asked himself, "What am I doing?" in the sense of wondering aloud whether he (and it was mainly "he") was making the best use of his finite time on earth, but in the literal sense, there was always an answer, the physical results in the actual world that verified that work had indeed taken place. By contrast, office work seems inherently precarious even in the absence of "headcount reductions"—it feels like getting paid for it can't continue forever, like someone is going to figure out what's going on and send you home.

In this context, it's particularly interesting that the *Office* is centered on a manager. Already in our discussion of the American version of the show, one can detect hints that the position of manager is intrinsically awkward: as soon as Michael, who seems like an inherently awkward person, leaves the office, his seemingly cool replacement Charles begins stoking up awkwardness of his own. Instead of playing the role of a referee who can defuse awkwardness, the manager becomes its central source. This makes sense when we consider the structure of white-collar work: if the workers are afflicted with a continual sense of their own futility, what can we say of the person who is supposed to direct their useless actions to their useless ends? The promotion to middle management doesn't solve the problem of vague office work, but redoubles it. (The only real solution is promotion to CEO, at which point the goal is absolutely clear: *loot!*) One is tempted to say that no matter how vague the task of management is, David Brent is obviously bad at it, but particularly in the second season, we are given to believe that he has somehow managed to achieve something. He boasts that he has increased profitability without firing any workers, for instance, and he is interviewed by a trade magazine, indicating that he has a good reputation in his field. And at the conclusion of the first season, when David and one of his peers compete for a promotion, David is the one who gets it initially—though he then fails the required health exam, meaning that his former colleague Neil is now his boss.

Neil is obviously meant to be a foil to David. He is young, good-looking, charming, and—crucially—actually funny. The two have to work together closely because Neil's former staff is being integrated into David's branch, and their one-sided rivalry produces some of the show's most painful moments. Among the worst (or best) comes during the initial meeting of the newly combined staff. David has of course prepared what amounts to an entire stand-up comedy routine to impress his new charges, but Neil speaks first, not only succeeding in eliciting the laughter David never manages to achieve, but even preempting some of David's own jokes. Nevertheless, David presses forward even with the redundant jokes, resentment clouding his already unreliable delivery, resulting in a stony silence among all concerned.

Alongside David, Neil's charm comes as a relief. Yet I think there is something slightly sinister about the character, precisely because he succeeds where David fails. If David is abusing his position in an attempt to be well-liked, is Neil being any less abusive simply because he manages to pull it off? No one wants to have David Brent as a boss, but he is little more than a failed attempt at the insidious figure of the "nice-guy boss"—the boss who insists he's your friend, who's affable and charming, who jokes around and keeps the atmosphere light, all the while maintaining the underlying hierarchy all the more effectively. David is especially awkward due to his poor execution, but the very role he wants to fill is intrinsically awkward because it attempts to artificially introduce friendship and equality where there is actually authority.

Fittingly, it is the successful "nice-guy boss" Neil who finally fires David, couching the entire thing in the euphemism of "offering a generous redundancy package" — even though it's an "offer" David must accept — and acting as though it was really David's idea that he is simply responding to. At first David is defiant, but when Neil and another higher-up come by later to finalize the arrangements, David openly begs not to be fired. The responses are suitably passive, claiming that "the wheels are already in motion" and dismissing David's refusal to accept the situation by saying it's not up to him. Neither manager ever quite claims responsibility for the decision, and to the very end, Neil wants to pretend that he's David's friend.

David's last-ditch attempt to beg for his job is one of the most touching moments in the show, but his very desperation seems to contradict my earlier claim that losing a vague office job contains an element of relief. I believe, however, that this contradiction ultimately points at a deeper contradiction in the very character of David Brent, his attempt to identify fully with his meaningless office job. This attempted identification is what makes the character so grotesque, because it is an attempt that necessarily fails: the vague office job is impossible to identify with, because when you push hard enough on that job, there's nothing there. David's exaggerated self-assurance, his hyperbolic gestures toward the "nice-guy boss" routine, his claims to be a renaissance man and his implicit claim that he has found a task worthy of a renaissance man — all of this is an elaborate defense mechanism. Paradoxically, these character flaws are the clearest possible evidence that he has really faced the void that is his job and turned away in fear.

What inspires that fear? It's the fact that he doesn't know what he's supposed to do. This isn't due to his own personal failings, but is inherent to the job—no one can know what a manager is supposed to do in this context, because there's nothing to do. The manager "manages" people who are doing nothing, insuring that they look busy all the while. Once you realize that this is the case, what is left other than self-aggrandizement and glad-handing, keeping up the scam until you can get to the next level?

The plot arc that leads to Neil's promotion is a key illustration. David continually talks about the profound solidarity he feels with his workers, but he applies for the promotion even though he knows that his office will be closed and merged with another one if he gets it. When he loses out as a result of the failed medical exam, he's back to his old tricks, loudly claiming that he turned down the promotion out of loyalty to his workers. One of the office workers catches him in his lie, but even if he hadn't, the whole thing doubtless would have come across as hollow opportunism anyway. On the other side, if David had gotten the promotion, his workers would have been angry at being forced to either move or endure a longer commute and been worried about possible redundancies, but could they have really blamed him for taking it? After all, had the medical exam turned out differently, it might have been David rendering Neil redundant instead of the reverse.

The question that naturally arises in the viewer's mind as all this unfolds is how David possibly could've beaten Neil out for the promotion in the first place. The surface-level answer is obviously to provide a plotline that sheds the worst possible light on David, but I would like to risk a more abstract interpretation that perhaps goes against the writers' conscious intentions but nevertheless seems to me to get at something important. There are two elements at play in this promotion:

his management prowess and, apparently totally separate from that, the pathology that prevents him from achieving the promotion once it's offered. On a more formal level, however, I believe that the same pathology is at work on both sides: his pathological overidentification with the role of manager, with all its hollowness and falseness, means that he really does deserve the promotion, yet it also renders him impossible to promote in practice. It's as though the organization can't admit that David Brent's obnoxiousness is what their system calls forth and yet can't deny it either, which is why they acknowledge David by offering the promotion to him first but nevertheless find a pretext to promote the more apparently "normal" Neil in his place.

In the end, then, David Brent's strategy to deal with the inherent awkwardness of his workplace proves to be just as fragile as Jim's in the US version of the show. The two can be seen as opposite extremes, with David choosing exaggerated overidentification and Jim choosing ironic detachment, but they both end in the same paradox: their very strategy for avoiding awkwardness turns out to be the cause of further awkwardness. David's strategy in fact leads to the most extreme reaction to awkwardness, namely the expulsion of the person who seems to be the cause. Jim also fears for his job for a time, and though Charles does begin to respect him toward the end of his time at the office, the only real solution to their tension is to get rid of Charles somehow. For good measure, once Charles leaves, he is retrospectively portrayed as the awkward person who was expelled.

Thus in both versions of *The Office*, we see at least some acknowledgment of one of the sinister reactions that awkwardness can produce, namely scapegoating and exclusion. Yet at the same time, both are asking us to laugh at awkwardness, to enjoy it. Does this mean that we should be suspicious of our enjoyment, wondering if it's tinged with an anticipatory joy at the excluded person's comeuppance? Do we enjoy awkwardness because we know that we will be able to join in the solidarity of, for example, knowing that Charles was just a big asshole all along? Here as usual, the original UK version provides greater nuance, asking us to identify with the person whose awkwardness leads to his exclusion—and to root for his re-inclusion in the context of the company Christmas party, itself surely one of the most awkward environments imaginable. Some might view this apparent "softening" of David Brent's character as something of a cop-out, but I think it gets at the hope toward which my argument is aiming: the hope for a solidarity based not on the overcoming of awkwardness, but on awkwardness itself.

Chapter 3

Cultural awkwardness—Judd Apatow

The previous chapter carried us through everyday awkwardness to cultural awkwardness, showing that the vaguely white-collar workplace that has become the norm for middle-class workers does not provide nearly a strong enough social order to stave off awkwardness and in fact directly generates certain forms of it. This chapter will deal with a setting that makes the workplace seem like a model of clarity, the Kafkaesque realm of contemporary marriage and coming of age. Every way we turn, it seems we're doing something wrong: putting off marriage too long, settling for the wrong person, getting married just for the sake of getting married, etc. Marriage itself seems to be in serious decline as an institution, with divorce an ever-present possibility and a kind of deadening routine threatening even the best marriages. In short, marriage has fallen into a state of cultural awkwardness.

This chapter will look at a series of films associated with the name of Judd Apatow, which fully admit to the cultural awkwardness surrounding marriage but nevertheless regard it as the only game in town. Focused on so-called overgrown adolescents who are, to varying degrees and for various reasons, putting off marriage indefinitely, these films despair of the possibility of developing any viable alternative to the shattered institution of marriage, proposing instead that we prop up the system by allowing reluctant men to indulge in the habits associated with the awkward status of overgrown adolescents as a kind of "release valve." I will be laying out the contradictions inherent in this solution, with particular emphasis on the question of how indulging in awkwardness can be a kind of reward for going along with the system when we normally regard awkwardness as precisely what the system exists to prevent.

The perils of being an overgrown adolescent

If Woody Allen was the king of awkwardness in 1970s American film, then Judd Apatow arguably fills that role now. There are some similarities between the two men: both are Jewish, both grew up in New York, both got their start in comedy at a comparatively young age, and both wrote for television before turning to film. The differences, however, are striking. Woody Allen has starred in the majority of his movies and in fact began directing in order to have control over his writing, to avoid the risk of other directors ruining his jokes. Over time, this led to the development of the so-called "Woody Allen character," who was easily identifiable even when Allen himself didn't star. By contrast, Judd Apatow has rarely acted, certainly never in a major role (though he has been hilariously funny in every interview with him that I've seen). In addition, he has most often served as a writer and producer rather than a director, but he filled all three roles in the two films that did the most to establish his name, *The 40-Year-Old Virgin* (2005) and *Knocked Up* (2007), as well as his most recent film, *Funny People* (2009).

Apatow's decision to stay out of the limelight has led to a strange phenomenon that also clearly distinguishes him from Allen: a certain slippage has occurred so that the name "Apatow" has come to designate not so much a man as a genre, such that movies that he is not directly involved in can somehow feel like an "Apatow film." This happens most often with movies starring key members of his acting ensemble, such as Seth Rogen or Jason Segel, but it has arguably reached the point where even that indirect connection is becoming unnecessary—for example, the 2009 screwball comedy *The Hangover* strikes me as being very much in the Apatow vein. What all these films share is an over-the-top form of comedy characterized by awkwardness, obscenity, and non-sequitur combined with a sentimental framing narrative that most often ends in marriage. At the very core of all of them, however, is a form of male bonding based not in traditional male activities like sports, but rather in the simple fact of being "overgrown adolescents," with all the marijuana, video games, and incompetent pick-up lines that status implies.

The fact that Apatow has most often chosen to focus on the overgrown variety of adolescents is interesting in light of his two short-lived TV series, *Freaks and Geeks* and *Undeclared*, which focused on actual adolescents (in high school and college, respectively). Both shows are remarkable for their honesty about the almost unbearable awkwardness that permeates one's adolescent years, an honesty that extends to the level of casting. Breaking with a long-standing TV tradition, Apatow's actors look like actual real-life teenagers, as opposed to the modelesque 20-somethings who usually populate high school sitcoms. It is easy for the TV viewer without much daily contact with teenagers to forget just how physically awkward they look, particularly the boys—and few have completely outgrown this gawkiness by the time they get to college.

In *Freaks and Geeks*, these casting decisions border on cruelty. Most significantly, the actor portraying the male lead, Sam Weir (John Francis Daley), was around fifteen in real life at the time and looked like a child, very short in stature without even the faintest indications of facial hair. The group of friends surrounding Sam's older sister Lindsay (Linda Cardenelli) were significantly older in real life, perhaps to make the age difference more apparent to the viewer, but they still looked like kids. Even the requisite "teenage heartthrob"

(James Franco) is clearly childish and a bit pathetic, a pattern that is repeated in *Undeclared*, where the good-looking male roommate at first appears to be a seductive "player" worthy of emulation but then proves himself to be insensitive and unable to sustain a relationship beyond one night. The films continue in this vein, undercutting good-looking characters and seeming to revel in the awkwardness of the flabby male body in particular, up to and including full-frontal nudity.

Just as in the case of Woody Allen, many critics have detected a misogynist edge in Apatow's oeuvre, but the ethos of the two bodies of work is significantly different in this regard. Where Allen is famously neurotic and seems to regard the figure of Woman as a kind of *mysterium tremendum*, equally frightening and fascinating, the misogyny of Apatow films is part and parcel of the homosocial environment of overgrown adolescents, as is the less-noted homophobia.

Though it may be a case of simply getting lucky—as one might say of the one unambiguously positive and strong Woody Allen woman, Mia Farrow's character in *Hannah and Her Sisters*—I think it's noteworthy that Lindsay, Apatow's one unambiguously positive and strong female character, appears in a teenage milieu. During adolescence, after all, everyone is testing the waters and dating seems both like one option among many and like a welcome change of pace from the homosocial adolescent diversions that may have already begun to feel forced. It can admittedly sometimes be difficult to tell how much difference it would have made if Lindsay had been male: the path she takes from goody-two-shoes to Grateful Dead follower (the show is set in the 1980s) could just as easily have been taken by a teenage boy. Yet that very fact arguably reflects the changes that feminism has brought about, an impression reinforced by the fact that the show is also very honest in dealing with the greater pressure that high-achieving girls like Lindsay often feel to be very "by the book" and with her and her parents' struggles with her path at a time when it was not yet self-evident that a girl would be well-served by going to college. Overall, though, one could say that Apatow can most easily portray a teenage girl positively because the entire setting renders her non-threatening.

For the *overgrown* adolescent male, however, things are more serious. Dating is no longer a harmless experiment—eventually the question of marriage will arise, and contemporary marriage is a frightening prospect. In part, this stems from the higher expectations of women now that a generation of strong, assertive women like Lindsay has grown up. Previously the system was, though obviously unjust from the woman's perspective, relatively simple for men to navigate: the man got to be in charge, and in exchange he provided for the woman. Now that women have claimed their right to self-determination, however, the situation becomes much less clear, and—most importantly—the inherent prestige that came along automatically with being a man has largely fallen by the wayside. Women are newly competent and self-assured, while men have followed the opposite trajectory. In short, men are expected to pursue women who all seem to be too good for them, in order to establish a partnership whose parameters are so vague as to virtually guarantee failure.

One can already see a hint of the difficulties in store in Lindsay's experiment with dating her friend Nick (Jason Segel), a relationship that incidentally produced one of the most painfully awkward moments ever committed to film, a scene in which Nick puts on the Styx song "Lady" and speaks the words along with the song as though it was a love poem he had written to her. Lindsay takes the lead in the relationship for the most part: she initiates the physical side of the relationship (on the night that Nick played the Styx song, all she wanted to do was make out) and also breaks it off when he becomes too smothering—or at least plans to break it off.

As it happens, in another terribly uncomfortable scenario, Lindsay confides in her mother about her decision to break up, and so, falsely assuming that the break-up has already occurred, her mother attempts to comfort Nick the next time she sees him.

Nick here represents many of the characters who will populate Apatow films: awkward, not particularly attractive, pursuing a "dream" (drums in this case) without any particular competence—someone who is dating far above his means. Being a teenager from an era before *Seinfeld*, Nick does not have the benefit of faux-ironic detachment and winds up heartbroken as a result. On the other side, Lindsey proves fairly resilient and is even willing to continue as seamlessly as possible as Nick's friend. This sharp contrast points to why I have chosen a body of work with such a relentlessly male perspective when there are so many shows that portray women's problems with our era's disjointed courtship routine, such as *Sex and the City* and *The Gilmore Girls* or, in an earlier era, *The Golden Girls*: women seem, by and large, to have displayed a basic social grace that allows them to deal with awkward situations relatively smoothly. If social awkwardness seems to be such a male-dominated field, it's because men have descended into self-pity, defensiveness, and even willful denial in response to their loss of relative prestige and the cultural awkwardness that followed.

Few of the later characters make themselves as vulnerable as Nick does, but his example leads one to suspect that the danger represented by the new post-feminist normalcy isn't simply a matter of the hero losing his "freedom." Instead, he puts off marriage because he is stuck in a situation of cultural awkwardness, one that he feels more acutely as a self-pitying man who is (mostly unconsciously) nostalgic for what being a man once meant. Marriage still seems like the only option, the only way to grow up, but marriage also somehow doesn't "work," it seems doomed to fail. Such is the difficulty of the overgrown adolescent's coming of age, the core subject matter of the Apatow-style film.

Marriage and family values for dummies

On the surface, Apatow films are very optimistic about marriage and coming of age. Aside from a handful of farces such as the parody music biopic *Walk Hard: The Dewey Cox Story*, one can say that the typical Judd Apatow film provides variations on the following basic plotline. We begin with an overgrown adolescent who is quite happy with his overgrown adolescent ways. Something unexpected then happens that makes him question his comfortable routine and aspire to adulthood. With much trepidation and many roadblocks along the way, he finally winds up married, a full-fledged member of the mature adult world.

In *The 40-Year-Old Virgin* and *Knocked Up*, the two films that I believe serve as the archetypes of the Apatow genre, this thread is clearly visible. *Virgin* finds Andy (Steve Carell) leading an essentially happy yet understandably tense life after failing to have sex for all of his forty years. He collects classic toys, all in their original packaging, and has a wide range of other hobbies that take up the excess energy his lack of sex leaves him. When his coworkers find out about his predicament, they are determined to end this epic dry spell. After a series of failed attempts, Andy finds his dream girl (Catherine Keener), eventually confessing his strange situation to her, leading her to (of course) accept him just as he is—and in the end, just for good measure, his freakish lifelong virginity proves to be no obstacle to amazing sexual prowess. In *Knocked Up*, Ben (Seth Rogen) lives with a bunch of guys who are assembling a website that indexes all the nude scenes in movies. He has a one-night stand with Alison (Katherine Heigl) and due to a miscommunication does not use a condom. She becomes pregnant and wants to keep it, and he decides to step up and become the father the baby needs. When Alison breaks up with him due to his insensitive slacker ways, Ben undergoes a massive transformation by means of a montage and returns as the perfect boyfriend who acquits himself well during the baby's birth, solidifying the unlikely relationship.

This structure echoes the classic coming-of-age story, but with one twist: our hero supposedly already *has* come of age, already is an adult. There is therefore something inherently awkward about the hero, an awkwardness that can only be abated by keeping to his circle of fellow overgrown adolescents as much as possible. Yet just as in the previous chapter, we find here that the strategy for avoiding awkwardness only winds up compounding it, as limited contact with the outside "normal" adult world leads the overgrown adolescent to underestimate the strangeness of his lifestyle. The initial encounter between Alison and Ben in *Knocked Up* is a case in point. Alison, like most Apatow heroines, is a fairly accomplished person by the time the narrative begins, having just secured an on-air role at E! Entertainment Television. She has yet to achieve full independence, living as she does with her sister's family, but she is far ahead of Ben, who takes advantage of an injury settlement he was awarded in order to sit around all day and do essentially nothing in the house he shares with his pot-addled friends.

When the two happen to go to the same club on the night Alison is celebrating her new on-air status, then, the audience is surprised, though not completely shocked, that she and Ben hit it off and have a one-night stand—after all, she is celebrating and wants to enjoy herself, and Ben is a nice enough guy. Yet Ben's isolation among his peers—especially given that Ben regards himself, with some justification, as "better" than them in many ways—allows him to seriously entertain the possibility that the two might have a future. It is this, rather than the simple disconnect between the two, that determines the degree of morning-after awkwardness the two experience. Waking up in bed with a stranger is always at least a little bit fraught, of course, but Ben makes things much worse by insisting that they hang out, apparently not even considering the possibility she needs to work. She agrees to get breakfast, but his choice of a run-down greasy spoon only highlights the incongruity. The breakfast is important to the plot insofar as it emboldens Ben sufficiently to give her his number—thereby enabling her to get in contact once she learns she's pregnant—but it also provides a healthy dose of awkwardness, as Ben digs himself ever-deeper into his hole. The very fact that Ben later claims he has blown his chance with her highlights his cluelessness: in any rational world, Ben had always already blown his chance.

As it turns out, however, Ben is not living in a rational world. In his world, a single career woman chooses to keep the baby she conceived with a total stranger—without acknowledging abortion as a live option or providing any type of reason for her choice. This strange unexplained decision is a hole at the center of Alison's character, rendering her little more than a narrative vehicle to bring about Ben's transition to adulthood. This is one of the things that opens up the movie to charges of sexism, including from the actress who played Alison, Katherine Heigl. Yet it also opens up a kind of fantasy world of further improbable consequences. For instance, Alison has obviously been chosen for on-air duty because of her "generically hot" look, and in the real world one assumes her pregnancy would result in her being returned to an off-camera role at best. Instead, her pregnancy winds up helping her career as women flock to her show. It helps Ben's career as well. When she breaks up with him after an improbably long attempt to "make it work," Ben—a man with no employment history who even claims to be an illegal immigrant (he's Canadian)—is able to find a nice design job in short order, moving into an apartment with a spare room for the baby. This show of responsibility lays the groundwork for Ben to help with the baby's birth and win Alison back in the process.

The speed with which Ben is able to join the adult world suggests a connection to another traditional genre in addition to the coming of age story: the fairy tale. It is as though becoming an adult is a magic power that the hero possesses without really knowing it—only in the crucial moment does he become aware of all he is capable of. The fact that Ben's transition occurs during a montage only heightens this connection, echoing the cliché montages of underdog characters undergoing hard training before a fight in which they are impossibly overmatched, a fight in which they inevitably prevail.

Here it is helpful to bring in an Apatow film that apparently falls outside the pattern I have identified: *Pineapple Express*. The main characters are Dale (Seth Rogen), a typical "loveable loser" character who makes his living serving subpoenas and is dating a high school girl, and his drug dealer Saul (James Franco). The two have an awkward relationship: Saul believes Dale is a close friend, while Dale is only interested in buying pot. Through a strange course of events, however, the two wind up on the run from the mob together. When they are inevitably caught, the pair gather up the courage and resolve not only to escape but to kill most of the mobsters and wind up blowing up the mob headquarters. In short, when the situation demands it, even a tubby process server and a skinny pot dealer can kick some serious ass.

On the one hand, then, getting your act together and getting married is presented as the easiest thing in the world. In an extreme case such as one sees in *The 40-Year-Old Virgin*, things obviously become more complicated, but even here the problem seems to be the tremendous hold Andy's overgrown adolescent (or even pre-adolescent) habits have on him after governing his life for such an extraordinarily long time. Once he lets go, the transition is seamless. On the other hand, though, the fact that this supposedly easy transition is presented in a format normally associated with fantasy paints a more ambiguous picture: is our hero's transition really any more believable than the *Pineapple Express* characters' immediate transformation into action heroes? If this is all taking place within the typically male frame of heroic fantasy, one is left with the question of whether these overgrown adolescents are *really* making any transition at all. This question can be asked in two respects, which I will treat in turn. First, is there really something there for them to transition *to*? Is there some viable way of living out the identity of "responsible married adult"? Second, do they ever really leave behind their awkward status of overgrown adolescents? The answer to both questions, as we will see, is no.

Yet another return of irony

As noted before, the overall narrative arc of these movies is an optimistic one, comedic in the classical sense, with their heroes rising from the lowly status of overgrown adolescents to the exalted office of responsible married adults. *The 40-Year-Old Virgin* couches this basic narrative in terms of overcoming the fear of embarrassment. After multiple improbable misadventures deprive Andy of several chances to lose his virginity, he reaches a point where he worries that women will be taken aback by the fact that he hasn't yet had sex, and that fear then sets off a vicious circle. Once his friends help him to overcome his fear, he winds up with the woman of his dreams in a "happily ever after" ending. *Knocked Up* also has what is formally a "happily ever after" ending insofar as the audience doesn't see the "morning after" with Ben and Alison—interestingly, however, the film implicitly interweaves the "morning after" narrative with the traditional wedding-bound narrative, in the form of the relationship between Alison's sister Debbie (Leslie Mann, Apatow's wife) and her husband Pete (Paul Rudd).

In a sense, the mismatch appears to be the opposite of Ben and Alison's: where Ben is too much of a loser for Alison, Pete is too cool for Debbie. He is witty, charming, and good-looking and has the almost farcically cool job of a talent scout for rock bands. Debbie, on the other hand, while very attractive—as a club bouncer reassures her in one of the most memorable scenes in the movie when he is constrained to keep her from entering due to her age—is portrayed as shrill and controlling, openly encouraging Alison to follow her example by "training" Ben to avoid all undesirable behaviors. Pete responds to her controlling ways by acting withdrawn, prompting Debbie to hold on tighter, resulting in a vicious circle, familiar from everyday life, that makes the couple very awkward in their interactions with one another and with the outside world.

Apatow explores this awkwardness in a way that shows him to have a much more profound grasp of the phenomenon than the writers for the US *Office*. This is particularly the case when he sets up the audience to suspect that Pete is having an affair and is therefore the unique cause of the awkwardness of the relationship by virtue of being an asshole. When Debbie notices that Pete seems to be sneaking around and leaving at odd hours, she recruits Ben and Alison to follow him to one of his liaisons. The bumbling crew manages to break into the house Pete has mysteriously entered, and when they barge into the room where one supposes Pete is engaged in foreplay, they instead find him huddled around with a group of guys, taking part in a fantasy baseball league draft. Of course we shouldn't be shocked that Pete isn't actually having an affair—in the Apatovian universe, the last thing men need is yet another woman to deal with. Nevertheless, Debbie, naturally unconscious of the genre she is a part of, is stunned that Pete would go to such great lengths to hide an innocuous pastime from her, and in the conversation that ensues, Pete reveals that his mysterious trips all feature similarly innocent behavior such as going to movies. He has no interest in an affair, but needs to create some space to keep Debbie from smothering him.

Once this is revealed, it becomes clear that Pete's withdrawn stance isn't the behavior of someone who has checked out of a loveless marriage, but instead represents a familiar strategy for dealing with awkwardness: ironic detachment. Rather than attempt to deal directly with his wife's demands, he tries to regard them with detached bemusement. In other words, the space he opens up by sneaking away is echoed in their face-to-face interactions. This is obviously the same strategy that Jim deploys in the US *Office*, but the stakes are much higher given that Pete is dealing with his wife rather than an oddball coworker like Dwight. In the emotional confrontation that follows Pete's confession, Debbie says something that many men of the post-*Seinfeld* generation (myself included) likely found difficult to hear: "You think because you don't yell, you're not mean. This is mean." Just as in Jim's case, the very strategy Pete uses to avoid the awkwardness of direct confrontation only makes things worse, as his nonchalant pose turns his every remark into a hurtful barb.

The example of Pete sheds light on the strategy of irony in general. Like Pete and like the *Seinfeld* cast, Jim is mean. Were Dwight to echo Debbie's accusation, it would immediately become clear that Dwight was in the right, because Jim's only possible retort would be that Dwight deserves to be mistreated because he's so weird. If we identify with his perspective, Jim's a witty and cool guy, whereas if we identify with the victim's perspective, Jim is a bully. Yet Apatow does not portray Debbie as simply an innocent victim. Pete isn't wrong to think of her as controlling, for instance, and it's not at all clear what he can do to keep her from acting that way. For her part, Debbie later admits that she feels insecure because Pete's life seems full of opportunity while she herself is on the downward spiral, above all because she believes her good looks are fading. Her attempts to control Pete could then be interpreted as a way to deal with her own feelings of vulnerability by setting up a reliable norm where Pete will give up on self-determination and become entirely dependent on her direction.

Both partners, then, are trying to avoid the awkwardness and unpredictability of direct and open communication with each other, Pete by constructing a contentless distance and Debbie by laying down the law—and just as in the previous chapter, their respective strategies for avoiding awkwardness only produce more awkwardness, in this case even mutually reinforcing each other. And once their strategies break down in the tense encounter that follows the discovery of the fantasy baseball draft, divorce seems to be the only option. Now one could claim that Pete and Debbie are a uniquely mismatched couple, but in the Apatow universe as in ours, every couple is mismatched. The problem, again, isn't simply with individuals, but with the social system itself: neither partner knows what they have the right to expect, but both feel like they *should* know. Pete and Debbie compensate for this uncertainty in opposite directions, by putting forth no expectations whatsoever and by excessively spelling out expectations, respectively, and this extreme unbalance is certainly especially problematic—but at the same time, there seems to be no proper balance, only degrees of imbalance.

Male bonding, the dangerous supplement

The solution that the family-oriented Apatow films propose is paradoxical: fight the inherent awkwardness of contemporary marriage with more awkwardness, specifically by injecting the awkwardness of the overgrown adolescent state into marriage itself. This accounts for the apparent contradiction in the films' treatment of their true subject matter, male friendship among overgrown adolescents, which serves as both a form of resistance to responsible married adulthood and as a kind of required transition into adulthood.

This second aspect is seen most clearly in *The 40-Year-Old Virgin*, where opening up and becoming "one of the guys" is a crucial step for Andy in his long-delayed quest for normality. One can also see it in the relationship between Ben and Pete in *Knocked Up*. After she learns that Pete has developed an elaborate space of secrecy in order to avoid her, Debbie wants to split up. Alison breaks it off with Ben shortly thereafter, and the two men take a trip to the Mecca of male bonding, Las Vegas, where they take magic mushrooms (a step above marijuana, the typical overgrown adolescent drug of choice) and eventually both decide that they want to win their respective women back—the "freedom" they experience in their return to overgrown adolescent status is not enough to make up for what they believe they've lost. More recently, the Apatow-style movie *I Love You, Man*, which did not involve Apatow himself but starred Apatow regulars Paul Rudd and Jason Segel, made this role of male friendship even more explicit: Paul Rudd's character has no close male friends, relying entirely on his fiancée for his social life, and feels he must find one to fill the role of best man so that he can have a normal wedding (and presumably a normal marriage—here, in contrast to *Knocked Up*, it is the woman who worries about being smothered). This film also makes it explicit that maintaining homosocial activities like the proverbial "poker night" is crucial to the success of a marriage.

At the same time, however, there's something utopian about male friendship. *Pineapple Express* displays this aspect perhaps most clearly, given that it focuses entirely on male friendship separated from the horizon of marriage. The two main characters form a bond that allows them to overcome even the most life-threatening obstacles, and a third character who betrays them is able to survive a truly excessive number of gunshot wounds once he joins their cause. Obviously this is all working on the level of fantasy, but it's worth attending to what that fantasy is saying: if we men remain true to each other, anything is possible. A similar dynamic is at work in *I Love You, Man*. After he makes friends with Jason Segel's character, a confirmed bachelor with a finished garage devoted to all the trappings of overgrown adolescence—ranging from a stage where they can pretend to be rock stars to a chair designated as the "masturbation station"—Paul Rudd's character finds a whole new range of possibilities opening up and experiences a much more intense bond than he appears to have with his fiancée. The friendship even threatens to derail the wedding, which in turn damages the friendship. Though everything of course turns out fine, it is noteworthy that the two reconcile in the context of the wedding ceremony itself, declaring their mutual love before the bride and groom exchange their vows. Clearly this friendship has exceeded its mandate as a preparation for normal marriage.

This utopian element is set in relief by *Superbad*, which centers on the friendship between high school seniors Evan (Michael Cera) and Seth (Jonah Hill). The narrative follows Evan, Seth, and their mutual friend Fogell (Chris Mintz-Plasse) as they attempt to fulfill their promise to bring beer to a party and thereby impress some girls. Over the course of the evening, tension builds between Evan and Seth as it becomes clear that Evan is going to room with Fogell at an exclusive college rather than joining Seth at a less-prestigious institution as the two had originally planned. In the end, all three wind up successfully seducing the girls of their dreams, but the really important declaration of love is that between Evan and Seth once their adventurous night is over, as they lay in sleeping bags in classic adolescent style—with Seth falling asleep with an arm draped over Evan.

The next morning, when the two meet their respective girls at the mall and walk off separately, Seth's longing to go back to how things were is palpable as he watches Evan walk away for an uncomfortably long time. Some have seen homoeroticism here, at least from Seth's side, an impression that is reinforced by a long, bizarre sequence earlier in the movie—so awkward it arguably begins to transcend the category of awkwardness—in which Seth randomly discloses that he got in trouble as a child for his fixation on drawing penises at every opportunity. I think that focusing too much on the homoerotic element misses the point, however. Seth is not putting his arm around or saying "I love you" to the Evan who is beginning to explore his sexuality, at least not consciously, but precisely to the Evan who is on the floor in a sleeping bag. He is trying to hold onto their specifically *adolescent* bond, which he had imagined would continue if they became college roommates. While *Superbad* is a variant on the quest narrative and therefore does include, to a lesser degree, some of the fantasy elements found in *Pineapple Express*, it is primarily Seth's melancholy that points toward the utopian aspect of male friendship—even if the loss of the adolescent homosocial bond is inevitable, it is a real loss, the loss of something really valuable.

What do these young men find valuable about their adolescent friendships, whether overgrown or age-appropriate? Above all, it seems that they value them for being more or less voluntary or spontaneous rather than rule-based. These friendships take time and effort to maintain, yet friends generally don't make *demands* in the same way that girlfriends and wives are portrayed as doing. Certainly there are some broad norms governing these friendships, such as loyalty or promise-keeping, but dwelling on those norms and their violation, as Seth does with regard to Evan's decision to go to the superior college, is somehow foreign to the way these relationships are supposed to work. In this sense, we could say that these friendships that take place during or mimic adolescence, the most intrinsically awkward period in a person's life, are themselves structurally awkward insofar as they fall outside any given set of recognized cultural conventions—but awkward in a good way, a promising way.

Here, in sharp contrast to the workplace environment, we can see that the imposition of the normality that dispels awkwardness is actually unwelcome insofar as the characters are attached to their awkwardness. And it is this embrace of the awkwardness implicit in adolescent homosocial friendships that explains the misogyny that many have seen in the Apatow genre: women represent the social ordering that is going to deprive men of their awkward adolescent bonds. Indeed, this may also explain the homophobia that's always simmering beneath the surface, because in the age of gay marriage (whether or not legally recognized), the horror is not so much the gay encounter as such, but rather the thought that this meaningful relationship could itself be submitted to the stereotyped conventions of marriage—a possibility that Seth's nagging already hints toward.

Abstracted from the misogyny, I believe that this embrace of the awkward, non-conventionalized relationship is something very valuable. But it is that very misogynist edge that makes this stance self-undermining, insofar as its very opposition to convention becomes itself a kind of negative convention—it becomes "just us guys" to the exclusion of everyone else. Once this move is made, it is possible to submit the entire circle of supposedly unique and authentic bonds between men to the needs of the very adulthood it resists, as a kind of "release valve." This is why male bonding can serve as a kind of initiation into responsible married adulthood: you need the supposedly authentic male bond to make marriage workable.

This is the paradoxical lesson of the Apatow genre: that the order of adulthood somehow doesn't work, that it needs the awkward supplement of the male bonding it supposedly overcomes. This is a despairing response to the failure of the 1960s revolution to produce a new positive vision for coming of age and living in community, resulting in a pervasive sense that despite the fact that we can never fully embrace the traditional norms, we are somehow hardwired to head in that direction and will do so immediately once our attempts to do something else fail. The way to live with the awkward, broken system that married adulthood has become is to redouble the awkwardness by making the utopian awkwardness represented by male bonding the servant of the very order it thinks it's fighting against.

There is one Apatow film, however, that begins to challenge this frame by finally portraying someone who tries and fails to achieve marriage and family: *Funny People*. This story of an aging comedian, played by and modeled after Adam Sandler, who is diagnosed with a terminal illness (and later cured) features an extended sequence—clumsily crammed into an already meandering and overlong movie—where the Adam Sandler character attempts to reunite with "the one who got away." He ultimately fails in his attempt to transcend his lifelong overgrown adolescence, not only because his lost love decides to stay with her husband but more fundamentally because even a short time with her children shows him he's no family man. Perhaps the movie would've been better if it had ended in that moment of despair, but what Apatow actually does is more interesting from my perspective: he portrays the Sandler character finding meaning in his relationship with a younger comedian (played by Seth Rogen, of course). This ending still falls within the general Apatow frame, portraying the so-called "bromance" as a consolation prize for someone who has lost his chance at the clearly superior option of marriage and family. Nevertheless, it marks a step forward, insofar as it is the first Apatow film other than the clearly fantasy-based *Pineapple Express* to portray awkward "male bonding" as an endpoint rather than a means of arriving at (or reinforcing) something else.

Overall, then, the Apatow genre's strategy is a step beyond the crass border control one detects in the brand of awkwardness practiced by the US version of *The Office*, but it tends to offer a rather perverse answer to the hope, implied by the original *Office*, that a solidarity based in awkwardness might be possible—after all, the normative social order itself is presented as inherently awkward, inherently breaking down, requiring a further dose of awkwardness to make it livable. Yet though the Apatow genre ultimately describes a social order that makes use of awkwardness to maintain itself, the films' clear desire for an adolescence that would be divorced from the horizon of adulthood points toward an awkwardness that would be embraced not in order to shore up something else, but solely for its own sake.

Chapter 4

Radical awkwardness—*Curb Your Enthusiasm*

My investigation of pop culture awkwardness began in the workplace, seemingly the perfect environment to study everyday awkwardness. I started with the common sense theory that awkwardness is generated by particularly awkward individuals and determined not only that awkwardness, as an inherently social phenomenon, cannot be limited to particular individuals but that the contemporary work environment was actually in a condition of cultural awkwardness and therefore awkwardness-generating. Moving on to the setting of marriage and coming of age, I looked at a common solution to the problem of cultural awkwardness, namely the use of awkwardness as a kind of "release valve" that helps make a crumbling system minimally workable.

In both cases, two patterns repeated themselves. First, it became clear that normal strategies for overcoming cultural awkwardness were ineffective. We can divide these strategies into two groups. On the one hand, there is escapism, represented by the pose of ironic detachment assumed by the US *Office's* Jim and *Knocked Up's* Pete. On the other hand, there is activism, seen in two variants: the UK *Office's* David Brent chose overidentification and its accompanying self-delusion, while *Knocked Up's* Debbie chose the attempt to "lay down the law" in the face of the uncertain norms of marriage. Neither the escapist nor the activist strategy proved stable, and in fact both strains were ultimately awkwardness-generating. This pattern helped to confirm my hypothesis, based on Heidegger, that awkwardness logically precedes every social order and can never be eliminated—no matter what strategy is used, it keeps coming back.

Second, despite the obvious discomfort associated with awkwardness, there was a tendency for awkwardness to become a site of utopian hope. In the original *Office*, that hope was centered on the reinclusion of David Brent in the office Christmas party, while in the Apatow universe, it attached to the bonds among awkward overgrown adolescents. This utopian element led ultimately to the question with which I will begin this chapter: if there is a sense in which we want awkwardness, then why should we have a social order at all? Answering it brings us beyond everyday and cultural awkwardness, which refer to a more or less stable norm, to the frontier of radical awkwardness, where there appears to be no norm governing the situation at all. My setting for this chapter is, at least initially, the realm of cross-cultural relations, which is the most common setting for radical awkwardness due to the lack of a third "meta-norm" governing interactions between adherents of two different norms. Just as radical awkwardness is more intense than everyday and cultural awkwardness, so is the strategy for dealing with it that will emerge in this discussion more thorough-going: namely, the attempt to get the disturbing foreigner to assimilate.

I have chosen Larry David's *Curb Your Enthusiasm* as my reference point here, leaving aside other more obvious options. I have done this first of all because Larry's travails as a New York Jew in Southern California illustrate very well the common-sense answer to this chapter's question: the reason we need a cultural norm is that the situation of radical awkwardness is unbearable. A second reason is the strange way in which this show recapitulates the themes of the previous chapters: he seems to be an inherently awkward person, for example, has a wife who acts as an enforcer of social norms, and takes refuge with a male confidant. Most importantly, however, I have chosen to conclude with Larry David because I believe he is the only one who provides us with a way forward, toward an awkwardness more radical than radical awkwardness itself—that is to say, toward a social bond based solely in awkwardness enjoyed for its own sake. Following the logic of "only Nixon can go to China," only Larry David, as seemingly the most awkward individual alive, can show us an awkwardness so joyously awkward that it becomes its own kind of grace.

This reflection on *Curb Your Enthusiasm* will also serve as the conclusion to this book, and as such, it will be somewhat different from the previous two chapters. On the level of the analysis of the show itself, things will remain very similar, but I will also be turning more explicitly to the kind of philosophical reflections that I undertook in the Chapter 1. Understanding that some readers' credulity may have been strained to the breaking point by my connection of Hegel and Heidegger to the question of awkwardness, I will be taking the risk of bringing Larry David into dialogue with an even more unlikely figure, but one who has become increasingly important for political philosophy in recent years: St. Paul the Apostle, who was active in the years immediately following Christ's death and did the most to spread his message, ultimately writing much of what would later become the New Testament. I turn to him not because of his theological commitments, but because of what his theological commitments led him to attempt to do, namely to found communities that include people from widely different cultures and yet don't require assimilation. My goal in referring to this unusual project is to make the case that Larry David has independently discovered something that St. Paul was experimenting with in the first century: how to form a community directly grounded in awkwardness.

A clash of civilizations

Curb Your Enthusiasm follows a slightly fictionalized version of Larry David, played by himself, through his day-to-day life in Los Angeles as he invariably offends his friends and acquaintances, most often played by themselves as well. The primary supporting characters are Larry's wife Cheryl (Cheryl Hines), his agent and confidant Jeff Green (Jeff Garlin), and Jeff's wife Susie (Susie Essman), and a wide array of supporting characters, usually celebrities playing themselves (such as Ted Danson, Wanda Sykes, and Richard Lewis), fill out their social circle. The fictionalization of Larry takes place in two directions: first of all, the early episodes make it clear that we are dealing with a version of Larry who has actually turned down the opportunity to make a show with HBO, so that the show is strangely premised on its own non-existence. Second, and perhaps relatedly, Larry David has clarified, during the course of an interview with Ricky Gervais (available on YouTube as of this writing), that the Larry who appears on-screen is purposefully made harsher and more difficult to get along with for comedic effect. In that interview, he tells Gervais that he draws many scenes from his everyday life, but with the twist that where the real-life Larry does the non-awkward thing, the on-screen Larry inevitably chooses the less socially graceful course.

In this respect, then, *Curb Your Enthusiasm* is also an exploration of everyday awkwardness, with Larry in the role of the graceless intrinsically awkward person—to such an extent that in the interview just cited, the real-life Larry David feels compelled to distance himself from his on-screen double: when Gervais asks him if he really acted as portrayed in a particular scene from the show, David responds, "Of course not—I'm not a sociopath!"

A more subtle source of awkwardness comes from the format of the show itself: David writes the overall stories to a certain degree of detail, but individual lines are improvised. In some cases, that leads to remarkable lines that probably wouldn't have arisen otherwise, as when Larry claims that his environmental activist's wife's choice of toilet paper is "like what you'd find on a whaling vessel"—disarming Jeff, who "breaks character" with his laughing repetition of the line. Most of the time, however, the result is a strange dialogue style that seems somehow less "realistic" than directly scripted dialogue would be. The interaction is staged, and all the participants know it, but they can't fully inhabit the characters they are supposed to play (who are in most cases themselves!) as they would be able to if they had preset lines to deliver. Real life and fiction become blurred, to the point where my above claim that Jeff "breaks character" in his spontaneous response to Larry's line becomes very difficult to adjudicate: what could breaking character possibly mean in this context? The characters are caught in a strange in-between space where their very lack of the normal apparatus of scripted acting calls even greater attention to the fact that they're acting—even at the nuts-and-bolts level, the situation is one of radical awkwardness, of falling between the cracks of two sets of norms (everyday spontaneous interactions and acting).

This radical awkwardness is also reflected on the level of the show's stories, which often focus on cross-cultural conflict. On the most obvious level, there are many episodes that focus on difficulties with people of other races, most often involving African Americans. To list just a few instances, there is an episode where Larry is shocked to hear a man in the bathroom use the "n-word" but can't seem to tell the story without a black person walking by and becoming outraged that Larry would use the word, one where he begins wearing bowties because he admires the bowties characteristic of the black Nation of Islam organization and is then dismissed as "Tucker

Carlson" (a Republican commentator) by a group of African Americans, and endless examples of the black comedian Wanda Sykes (a close friend of his wife) berating him for virtually anything he does when interacting with a black person. Other racial conflicts come into play as well, as when Larry mistakenly believes that his Korean bookie has kidnapped Jeff's dog in order to eat it.

Yet the more interesting cultural conflict is less noted: the conflict between Larry's New York Jewish culture and the passive-aggressive culture of southern California "WASPs" (White Anglo-Saxon Protestants). Though Larry is certainly guilty of instigating a great deal of everyday awkwardness, it is this cross-cultural encounter that creates the majority of the show's conflict. The reason this conflict is so strong is the same reason that it's so difficult to see: both Larry and the other participants are, with a few exceptions, culturally coded as "white." Everyone therefore expects Larry to be an insider to their culture, making his constant lapses incomprehensible and inexcusable. In more straightforward cases of radical awkwardness, one is normally prepared to cut the foreigner some slack or at least anticipates awkwardness—here one might detect a positive impulse in the example of midwestern Americans who try to speak slowly to foreigners—but in this case, radical awkwardness is misinterpreted as everyday awkwardness, and Larry's relative isolation among members of southern California culture (even his wife is a WASP) makes him seem increasingly like an intrinsically awkward person. Ultimately, when his wife divorces him in the sixth season, he becomes a total social pariah as one friend after another shuns him, explaining, "We're going with Cheryl" (the only exception being Jeff and Susie, who are also Jewish).

The fact of being an outsider who is misread as an insider causes Larry enough trouble, but the problem is compounded by the fact that southern California culture, at least as portrayed in the show, seems especially inscrutable, filled with bizarre rules that "you're just supposed to know." For instance, in one episode the actor Ben Stiller invites Larry to his birthday party but strongly emphasizes the fact that he doesn't want a present. When Larry accordingly shows up with no gift, Stiller is outraged, claiming that everyone should know that his claim not to want a present wasn't intended to be taken seriously. On another occasion, Larry gets take-out from a Chinese restaurant that mixes up his order with a friend's. When they return to the restaurant and exchange orders, Larry finds that his friend has taken most of the shrimp from his meal and is understandably upset—he complains to everyone who will listen, but everyone responds in the same way: "everybody steals shrimp." A similar situation arises in connection with his dry cleaner: when they lose a garment of his, they claim that's just the way it goes and that eventually he'll get someone else's garment, so that everyone will come out even in the long run. Larry takes his battle for a more common-sense system where everyone gets their own garments to Senator Barbara Boxer (played by the actual senator), who not only repeats the same thing Larry has heard from everyone else but reveals that the dress she is currently wearing mysteriously showed up in her dry cleaning one day. Larry's stubbornness makes him slow to adapt, admittedly, but it is clear that he faces an uphill battle in adapting to a culture that is exceptionally dense with unspoken rules.

Larry David and St. Paul

While there are obviously factors that make it unusual, Larry's situation in Los Angeles is an example of the more general problem of assimilation, which I already mentioned in the first chapter as a possible response to the anxiety produced by radical awkwardness. In many respects, *Curb Your Enthusiasm* provides an especially fruitful example of this problem. In the first place, the demand for assimilation in Larry's case is hugely intensified by his friends' belief that he shouldn't need to assimilate at all, which in turn intensifies his feeling of exclusion beyond what a white American moving into another circle of white Americans would normally feel. In addition, the show tends to isolate the cross-cultural conflict from all other concerns, given that Larry is fabulously wealthy due to the success of *Seinfeld* and moves among entertainment elites, so that usually no one involved faces serious economic or practical difficulties.

Another consequence follows from the extreme wealth of most of the characters: the stakes of everything they do are incredibly low. Most of the time, they are simply trying to have fun. The fact that nothing that occurs in any of the episodes is particularly important makes the anger of the people Larry comes in contact with seem all the more disproportionate—if everyone is just trying to have a good time, why ruin a pleasant evening because of one faux pas on Larry's part? It's as though the lack of any economic or other practical worries frees everyone to police Larry's behavior all the more strictly. Larry can certainly be as petty and insensitive as the next person, but most often, particularly in the early seasons, the viewer feels that Larry has a point. For instance, in the case of Ben Stiller's birthday party, it seems insane to have a convention of insincerely insisting that no one bring gifts when gifts are clearly expected. In most cases, his wife Cheryl insists that he apologize for his lapse later, leading Larry to begin an apology but then attempt to reason with the person and get them to admit he wasn't entirely in the wrong—a strategy that invariably makes things worse.

At the risk of being culturally insensitive, I would propose that the extreme reactions to Larry's behavior reflect his social circle's sense of cultural superiority: they are the elite of the entertainment industry, they are wealthy, they hold all the correct liberal opinions, and therefore their ways are not to be questioned—even on the relatively innocuous level of proposing that another way of doing things might make sense. This self-satisfaction comes up again and again in the series. For instance, in the same episode when Larry is having such difficulty with his dry cleaning, he attends an event at a museum to which he has donated an entire wing, but he is upstaged by another donor who wished to remain anonymous. It quickly becomes clear that the donor is none other than Cheryl's friend Ted Danson, who has told all his friends about the anonymous donation he just made. Larry points out—as any right-thinking person would agree—that Danson is missing the point of an anonymous donation by making his supposed selflessness known. Cheryl confirms this point when she explains that Danson typically makes anonymous donations and then tells others about it "to feel better about himself." Oblivious to the contradiction she has herself exposed, she remains deeply impressed at his generosity and selflessness. The double standard is clear: Larry can't do anything right, while the insiders can do no wrong.

It is here that I would like to follow up on my earlier references to Hegel and Heidegger by making another unexpected connection: namely, between Larry David and St. Paul. I want to focus on one of the most contested passages in Paul's writings, found in the seventh chapter of the Epistle to the Romans. Writing in the first person, Paul describes not only the apparent impossibility of keeping the law, but more radically seems to be claiming that the law directly causes its own violation. It is difficult to know what to make of this passage. Is Paul speaking only of the Jewish law, or of law in general? Is he talking about his own personal experience? If not, then whose? Most interpreters, following St. Augustine and Martin Luther, tend to interpret the passage as showing the inner conflict of every human being, who is unable to do good on his own and must trust in God's grace. They tend to agree that Paul is speaking about the Jewish law in particular, but believe the point can be generalized to all religious systems, none of which can provide a way to God independently of God's own initiative.

I would not want to be seen as attempting to overthrow such a long-standing theological tradition in the context of a book about sitcoms and comedy movies, yet the mark of a culturally significant text is that it invites many different readings. After watching *Curb Your Enthusiasm*, I began to think of the passage differently, viewing it through the lens of Paul's mission in life: trying to figure out a way to create communities that crossed the biggest cultural line that he was aware of, that between Jews and Gentiles, with everyone participating as equals. While contemporary Judaism is not a missionary religion, various first-century versions sought converts and were actually quite successful, as many in the ancient world found Judaism's ancient pedigree and strict morality very attractive. Paul eventually became convinced, however, that the coming of Christ meant that the wall between Jews and other groups needed to be torn down and that Gentiles needed to be able to participate in community with Jews, but without first becoming Jews.

That mission to bring together Jews and Gentiles is what he is attempting to explain and justify in the Epistle to the Romans, rather than any kind of general theory of human nature—and so I would propose that perhaps the chapter in question actually refers to the struggle of a Gentile trying to become a Jew, a situation with which he empathizes so strongly that he speaks in the first person on behalf of the Gentile convert (speaking in multiple voices being a common rhetorical technique in the ancient world). The law that constantly trips up the speaker isn't the Jewish law as such. After all, those who are born and raised Jews manage to follow it without any great difficulty, and Paul even says in another epistle that he was able to follow it perfectly. Rather, it's the Jewish law viewed from the perspective of a convert. Things that once seemed unproblematic, such as eating certain foods, are now forbidden—and it's easy to see how one could become so frustrated that one would want to eat pork, for example, simply out of rebellion against what seem like unreasonable demands.

The convert obviously admires the culture he's trying to join, but at the same time it seems to trip him up constantly. No matter how hard he tries, no matter how long he's a part of the new community, he will never be able to fulfill the law's demands as easily and fluently as someone who's been a member since birth—and so no matter how much his new community respects him and bears with his struggle, he will always be second best. In assimilation, the larger community takes care of the awkwardness it experiences in dealing with a foreigner in their midst, but only by "off-loading" all the awkwardness onto the convert. As with the other strategies, then, assimilation doesn't get rid of awkwardness, but only moves it around, producing the danger that it will re-erupt without warning—a possibility that Larry's experience illustrates, as it seems clear that much of his awkward stubbornness stems from his frustration at being constantly corrected and forced to apologize when he's done nothing he considers wrong.

This interpretation, grounded as it is in Paul's specific context, perhaps paradoxically seems to be more generally applicable than the interpretation that assumes he's talking about humanity in general. After all, most people aren't aware that they're struggling with sin and the impossibility of doing good unless a Christian comes along and tells them they are, but everyone who's tried to assimilate to another culture can relate to the feeling of never being able to fully become an insider. Though he is not consciously trying to "convert" to become a southern Californian, Larry still feels these same pressures as he tries to live his daily life among his very self-satisfied and judgmental community—and so we can perhaps dare to say that St. Paul was speaking to Larry David's situation as well.

Enjoy your awkwardness!

What motivates this reference to St. Paul, however, is not simply his analysis of the pitfalls of assimilation—it is a common enough problem, and many others have discussed it in more accessible terms. Rather, I am interested in the practical solution he offers, which is best seen in light of what he rejects. Clearly he rejects assimilation, because he believes it can never be a basis for a community where everyone participates on equal footing. If we assume for the moment that Paul is logically consistent, the rejection of assimilation also entails the rejection of another possible solution: creating some new third culture that everyone involved can "convert to." Such a solution is inherently unstable, because once a new generation of children is raised up in the new culture, the problem of assimilation simply repeats itself for any outsiders who subsequently want to join. One can see this pattern in the history of Europe: the secular state was devised as a kind of common space where people of differing religious sects could meet, but once it became established, it had difficulty incorporating people from other religious groups and sometimes even defined secular culture as opposed to those groups (particularly Islam). The first generation may be able to participate in the newly-developed culture as equals, but it is difficult to imagine every generation having the patience to keep developing entirely new cultures—if they want to live with people from other cultures, assimilation will seem like the only solution, and if they don't, exclusion, expulsion, or even extermination may become tempting options.

The solution Paul proposes, then, is to stop looking for a solution. No one should be forced to conform to the arbitrary social norms of others, and at the same time, everyone should feel free to maintain their cultural identity—Jews remain Jews, with all that means, and Gentiles remain Gentiles, without converting to some third thing. Instead of trying to come up with some permanent way of overcoming awkwardness, one should *go with it*. What this means in practice is that one should do the opposite of what the strategy of assimilation demands: rather than making the weaker ones (the numerical minority, the socially graceless, the disadvantaged) conform to the dominant group, the stronger ones should do their best to accommodate those who are having difficulty.

Though he gets very little credit for it, I believe that Larry very often follows this principle—perhaps due to the constant mistreatment he receives from his high and mighty friends, Larry is very generous to those whom others tend to forget about or even shun. In fact, many of his difficulties stem not from his lack of social grace, but from his over-generosity. One recurring character, for example, is a blind man who continually takes advantage of Larry. When they first meet, the blind man recruits Larry and his friend Richard Lewis to help him move into a new apartment, claiming that it will only take a few minutes. Naturally it takes all day, leaving the already underdressed Larry looking so sweaty and dirty that he is mistaken for a homeless person and kicked out of a jewelry store where he intended to buy something to placate his ever-demanding wife. Later they meet again, and when Larry's misplaced honesty leads him to tell him that his girlfriend isn't as attractive as she claims to be, the blind man breaks up with her and then guilts Larry into waiting on him hand-and-foot like the girlfriend used to. On another occasion, he befriends a new neighbor who turns out to be a registered sex offender, and everyone is outraged when Larry feels he can't exclude him from a party to which the whole neighborhood is invited. Even when it isn't strictly a matter of generosity, Larry seems more comfortable among outcasts, as when he hires a prostitute solely so that he can use the carpool lane and get to a sporting event on time—they wind up spending the entire evening together, and he clearly gets along better with her than with any of his uptight friends.

Even this guideline fails to become a reliable norm, however, because St. Paul makes it clear that who is weak and who is strong will vary by situation. Instead of a rule, one might call the principle of favoring the weak a *style* of inter-action, a starting point for social improvisations. This improvi-sation doesn't overcome the awkwardness of cross-cultural interactions, but dwells in it—and by leaving everyone's pre-existing cultural expectations alone, it dwells in awkwardness in a way that is remarkably different from the "release valve" strategy enjoyed by Judd Apatow's overgrown adolescents. Awkwardness is no longer a way of escaping social norms, and social norms are no longer a way of escaping awkwardness: instead, people simply meet each other, without the mediation of a defined cultural order, and figure out how to live together on a case by case basis. It is difficult to envision what these communities looked like in practice, and Paul's letters don't provide much help, focused as they are on the difficulties and conflicts that inevitably arose. Yet people nevertheless continued to attempt to make these communities work, which means that there must have been something attractive and convincing about the way of life Paul was advocating.

While we don't now have access to the particular forms these communities took, I do believe that we can experience what made these communities so appealing: all we need to do is rent the DVDs of *Curb Your Enthusiasm* season 3. At first glance, the situation could not be further removed from Paul's communities, which were made up mostly of the down and out: Larry and his wealthy friends are trying to start up a restaurant, basically as a hobby. As always, nothing goes right for Larry—he alienates a major food critic, along with several potential head chefs—and everyone soon comes to believe that he is going to wind up torpedoing the entire project. He saves the day by tracking down a great French chef, but unfortunately it turns out that the chef has Tourette's syndrome, causing him to shout out obscenities at random (in English, curiously enough) without even realizing he is doing so. The restaurant has been designed so that the chef will be in constant view and there is no time to change things before the scheduled opening, and so the other partners want to fire him—but the chef's tattoo of a string of numbers leads Larry to conclude that he must be a Holocaust survivor, and he insists that they can't possibly fire a Holocaust survivor. The other partners agree, deciding that they can only hope that he won't have an outburst during business hours.

It should be clear by now that the show's world is structured in such a way that the chef absolutely must have an outburst on opening night. What is interesting and surprising is Larry's reaction to the outburst, and to understand it, it's necessary to look back at two previous scenes. The first takes place within the overall restaurant plot without being closely connected to it. One day, Jeff is driving Larry around and needs to stop at his daughter's school, where they see that most of the boys are shaved completely bald. When Larry asks what's going on, Jeff says that one of the students has been diagnosed with cancer and is undergoing chemotherapy, and so the others have shaved their heads in solidarity with him. Larry is deeply moved—perhaps because no one has ever cut him any slack in any of the show's episodes—and repeats several times that he hopes he can do something so generous some day. The other scene occurs on the day that the restaurant opens. Larry asks the chef how he's doing and he responds that he's doing terrible: he has just lost the lottery by only one number, after playing the same numbers for many years. In the course of the conversation, he even decides to give up on this combination of numbers and, licking his finger, he wipes off the numbers on his arm—what Larry thought was a concentration camp tattoo was actually nothing but a set of lottery numbers written in pen. The entire rationale for keeping the chef despite his Tourette's syndrome is therefore gone, but it's too late to fire him, as the restaurant opens in only a few hours.

When the chef inevitably yells out his obscenities, the previously bustling restaurant falls silent and all the owners look at each other in shock. Thinking back on the bald high school students, Larry realizes that he has his chance to do something equally generous. In the ultimate act of identifying with the awkward person, Larry yells out his own string of obscenities. The other owners decide to follow suit, each in a way that reflects their own personality—Jeff, for instance, simply shouts, "Cock! Cock! Jism!" while an uptight person uses milder words like "darn" and "crap." Soon everyone in the restaurant is joining in and having a great time. Jeff's wife Susie walks into the middle of it, just as Cheryl is yelling out "motherfucking bitch." Susie takes it personally—Cheryl had strained their friendship after breaking a series of lunch dates, most recently when she had to get out of the car in the middle of a carwash because a "colon cleanse" rendered her incapable of controlling her bowels—and in one of the greatest achievements in the history of improvisational comedy (David assures Ricky Gervais that this line was not scripted), she responds to Cheryl's perceived insult by saying, "Fuck you, you fucking carwash cunt!" Even though motivated by enmity, Susie is drawn into this scene of joyous awkwardness and, like everyone else, participates voluntarily and in her own way.

This brilliant scene marks the end of the season: for once, Larry has succeeded, because of his awkwardness rather than in spite of it. It's a clear example of accommodating the person who is causing awkwardness rather than shunning or shaming them, but at the same time, it's as far as possible from the self-denial and asceticism we often associate with helping out the lowly—it's hard to imagine anyone watching this scene without being won over, without at least a part of them wishing they could have been there. The chef's outburst opens up a gap in the social order and Larry's identification with him only exacerbates things, and yet everyone involved is somehow much more comfortable than they would have been if things had gone as expected. More than comfortable, they're joyous, fully alive. If this kind of joy is what results when we identify with awkwardness rather than trying to fight it, then it's no wonder people found St. Paul's mission so appealing.

Here a possible objection arises: sure, this looks like great fun, but does it point toward anything sustainable? With regard to this particular scene, the show is little help, ending (*Seinfeld*-style) in the middle of the torrent of curse words and never bringing up the restaurant again in future seasons. The ending of the fourth season, however, is structurally very similar and may help to shed some light on this question. The primary plot arc of the season has Mel Brooks calling on Larry to star in *The Producers*. As always, Larry seems to destroy everything he touches, alienating one co-star (Ben Stiller) to such a degree that he quits and almost doing the same with his replacement (David Schwimmer). Yet all his other failings fade into the background when he draws a total blank on a line that is literally nothing but a summary of the musical's premise (that it's theoretically possible to make more money on a flop than a successful musical). Schwimmer tries to feed him his line, but to no avail, and the silence is only broken by Larry's oddball cousin, who picks that moment to ask the turbaned man in front of him to move over so he can see. Larry seizes on the distraction to do an impromptu stand-up comedy routine, winning the audience back and giving himself time to think of the line.

Here again, going with his awkwardness pays dividends: the show becomes a huge hit. The really funny thing, however, is that Mel Brooks and his wife leave while Larry stands silent and in their conversation reveal that Larry's screw-up was all part of the plan. Knowing that Larry was a walking disaster, they casted him in *The Producers* because they were tired of doing it and, in yet another example of pre-90s irony, wanted it to flop. While Larry's move might initially look similar to the Apatovian strategy of indulging in awkwardness in order to prop up the social order, in the context of Brooks' plot, it seems justifiable to say that Larry's success is of a subversive kind — a success based in the solidarity of awkwardness he formed with the audience rather than in his talent as a performer.

The clearest example of a longer-term community of awkwardness, however, is found in the sixth season. The most notable plot point of this season is Cheryl's decision to divorce Larry, but there is an additional overarching plot based on Cheryl's insistence that they take in a family of African Americans from New Orleans who have lost their home in a fictionalized version of Hurricane Katrina. Awkwardly named the Blacks — on meeting them, Larry remarks, "That'd be like if I was named Larry Jew!" — the family consists of Loretta, a single mother, her two children, and her Auntie Rae. They are soon joined by Loretta's brother Leon, who moves in with the Davids despite already living in Los Angeles. Conflict begins almost immediately when Jeff orders a cake for a party at the Davids that is (unbeknownst to Jeff) shaped like a huge black penis, continuing through a series of misunderstandings that make Auntie Rae think Larry is sexually harassing her, and culminating when Loretta overhears him telling the aforementioned story featuring the "n-word" and moves in with Jeff and Susie instead—only to move back in without comment when it turns out that Jeff snores too loudly for them.

Over time, however, Larry develops a real bond with the Blacks, especially with Leon, who becomes a confidant figure and, more importantly, a consistent advocate and defender. When Larry loses his clothes at the dry cleaner, Leon confronts someone who seems to be wearing Larry's shirt and takes it from him; when Larry goes to the doctor with intense crotch pain, Leon is there to help him deal with the diagnosis of unusually "long balls." As all of his other friends abandon him in the wake of the divorce, the Blacks become an increasingly important support system for Larry, and when they announce that their house has been rebuilt and they can return to New Orleans, he is visibly shaken.

The night before the Blacks are to leave, Larry is invited to a wedding that Cheryl will also be attending and invites Loretta to be his date. They end up having a wonderful time and are portrayed waking up in bed together—after which there is a montage that shows them getting married and enjoying various family activities together. Key themes that emerge in this montage are support, as when Loretta defends him against a pushy friend rather than setting him up for failure as Cheryl always does, and unselfconscious flouting of social expectations, as for example when Larry joins in with the Blacks as they (following a widespread American stereotype) talk and laugh loudly at the movies. Larry and the Blacks become a kind of community of exiles, bound by their shared condition of being awkwardly thrown into a social milieu where they don't belong, freeing each other to be themselves in an otherwise constraining and judgmental environment.

The utopia of everyday life

When I first watched the episode that ends with that montage, I wasn't sure whether I was supposed to take it as Larry's fantasy or as actually taking place within the show's reality. The new season has just begun as of this writing, and it is clear that it was real and that things have not gone as smoothly as the montage would lead one to believe. Nevertheless, I think it's helpful to dwell with the ambiguity that attends the introduction of this strange community of Larry David and the Blacks, because the ambiguity itself tells us something important about the solidarity of awkwardness. Yes, it is a fantasy, first of all because it seems so attractive—almost too good to be true. It feels as though it can't really work—is Larry really in love with Loretta or just afraid to be alone? will the Blacks really tolerate his neurotic ways once they're no longer simply guests in his house? etc.—and yet it feels as though if it did work, it would *really* work, as though one is witnessing the shift whereby the most improbable solution turns into the only solution possible.

With this in mind, I would like to return to my observation in Chapter 1 about the word "awkward" itself: if "awkward" is etymologically a directional term like "forward" or "backward," then where is it pointing us? I began by pointing out that "awk" seems to indicate that something has gone awry and proposed that that "something" had to do with the social order. In the meantime, my analysis has pushed beyond the complex relationship between awkwardness and more or less stable systems of social norms, toward a place where awkwardness can be openly embraced for its own sake. The direction awkwardness has in fact taken us, then, is beyond the common sense notion of awkwardness as a disturbance in the social fabric and toward something like utopia.

In retrospect, utopia was always an awkward place, with its famous two-faced etymology that renders it paradoxically both the good place and no place at all. I've already explored the ways that awkwardness can be a good place in sufficient detail, but what is one to make of the notion of "no place"? I would argue that awkwardness shows us that utopia is "no place" in an unexpected sense. It is "no place" because there's no need to go anywhere: the utopia of awkwardness is where we already are. Rather than an ideal order that must be established, it is a strangely inverted kind of utopia that all of our social orders try and fail to *escape*.

Here one must reject the core presupposition of the liberal political theory that has shaped the modern world. These theorists, such as Hobbes, Rousseau, and Locke, have proposed that the problem is to find a way to bind isolated individuals together, and their proposed solutions have focused on the idea of freely-entered contracts—all of society, up to and including the origin of government, can be understood in terms of individuals leaving behind their isolated state and freely making mutually beneficial agreements. What the analysis of awkwardness shows us is that the real problem is instead how to cope with the often overwhelming and always unavoidable proximity of others. The insight of the naïve reader approaching the foundational texts of modern political theory is helpful here, because common sense tells us that human beings don't, as liberal theory seems to presuppose, sprout out of the ground and only later encounter each other. Rather, we come into this world in a state of irreducible dependence, unceremoniously pushed or cut out of another person with whom we subsequently have a relationship (even if a negative one of absense) that we will never fully come to terms with, never be able to submit to clear concepts or rules. Such is the joy and burden of being human—we will never really be free individuals freely entering into contracts. As Heidegger tells us, we are "thrown" into this world, which means being thrown into our relationships as well.

It is easy to see how this fact can be intimidating, just as it is easy to see how isolation, including the regulated isolation that we call society, can be seductive. Yet looking at it positively, what this means is that gaining access to this utopia of mutual enjoyment—unmediated by those social orders that in the last analysis serve only to separate and exclude—is simple: we just need to admit to ourselves, and induce others also to admit to themselves, that it is where we already are. The examples from *Curb Your Enthusiasm* show us the basic pattern. Rather than attempting to cover over the gap introduced by the eruption of awkwardness, one should endorse it by redoubling it, and rather than minimizing its impact by "covering" for the person who has caused the awkwardness, one should expand its scope. The pattern is clear in both the *Producers* and the restaurant plotlines, but for me the restaurant scene is much more radical because Larry is not redoubling his own awkwardness but joining in someone else's, meaning that the fundamentally social nature of awkwardness is consciously chosen and endorsed as well. In its turn, the relationship between Larry and the Black family brings out the fact that awkwardness is a social bond that exists outside the social order, insofar as they have nothing in common aside from the fact of being thrown into a social order where they can never fully belong.

This immediacy of the utopia of awkwardness also cuts against key assumptions of revolutionary leftist practice, which has argued for a gradual process to reach the utopia of "from all according to ability, to all according to need." One cannot simply jump to communism, Lenin claimed, but must work through the dictatorship of the proletariat (in the form of its party), phasing out capitalism generation by generation as each new cohort is raised up with progressively better ideals and expectations. At first glance, this strategy does show a certain realism. Yet we can only learn by doing, and there is no one who can "practice" steering an entire civilization in the right direction over the course of generations. What we *can* do, however, is practice the skill of awkward improvisation, of identifying those situations most fruitful for intervention, of feeling out the shape and rhythm of consciously-chosen redoubled awkwardness. Practicing that set of skills would be a unique kind of "revolution" in that we'd already be enjoying the end result even as we're trying to bring it about.

Such a practice is perhaps too modest to have much large-scale effect, and it is far from certain that any enduring form of life will emerge out of it—indeed, the social order may well prove flexible enough to co-opt this particular form of awkwardness just as it co-opts the awkwardness of "overgrown adolescents." If a particular practice of awkwardness is reintegrated into the social order, however, that's all for the good—the practice of radical awkwardness is not defined by opposition to the social order for the sake of opposition, and any social order that makes more room for awkwardness is thereby making more room for human beings.

In any case, opportunities to enjoy the community of awkwardness are always there, always available, always ready to erupt, because awkwardness is undefeatable. Social orders arise and perhaps evolve and eventually fall, but awkwardness will endure as long as we remain human because it is what *makes* us human. What Ricky Gervais and Judd Apatow point toward and Larry David practices is indeed an awkwardness so awkward it becomes its own kind of grace—it is the peculiar kind of grace that allows us to break down and admit that we are finally nothing more or less than human beings who will always be stuck with each other and, more importantly, to admit that we are glad of it.